This book was conceived, edited and designed by

McRae Publishing Ltd, London

www.mcraepublishing.co.uk
Publishers Anne McRae, Marco Nardi

Project Director Anne McRae
Art Director Marco Nardi
Photography Brent Parker Jones
Text Carla Bardi
Editing Leanne Earwaker, Daphne Trotter
Food Styling Lee Blaylock
Food Preparation Lute Clarke, Pierrick Boyer
Layouts Aurora Granata
Prepress Filippo Delle Monache

NOTE TO OUR READERS
Eating eggs or egg whites that are not completely cooked poses the possibility of
salmonella food poisoning. The risk is greater for pregnant women, the elderly, the
very young, and persons with impaired immune systems. If you are concerned about
salmonella, you can use reconstituted powdered egg whites or pasteurized eggs.

ISBN 978-88-6098-327-5

Printed in China

CARLA BARDI

MEAT

200 SIMPLE & SUCCULENT RECIPES

mc
rae
PUBLISHING

contents

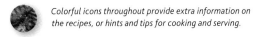

Colorful icons throughout provide extra information on the recipes, or hints and tips for cooking and serving.

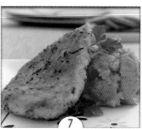

1
chicken kebabs
with lemon & herbs

2
chicken kebabs
with soy & cilantro

3
chicken with lemon
& caper sauce

TOP
20

4
grilled chicken
with figs & feta cheese

5
grilled chicken
with lemon, garlic & tomatoes

6
duck yakitori with scallions

7
crumbed turkey with sweet
potato mash

8
sautéed turkey
with marmalade glaze

9
veal escalopes
with pizza topping

10
veal escalopes with arugula,
parmesan & balsamic vinegar

11
veal escalopes with tomatoes,
eggplant & cheese

veal escalopes with lemon

chicken & broccoli stir-fry

thai beef stir-fry

quick recipes

pork escalopes
with marsala wine

grilled pork
with bean salad

grilled pork
with sage & lemon

parmesan veal rolls

roasted chicken rolls
with cheese

chicken rolls
with pancetta & parmesan

1 chicken kebabs
with lemon & herbs

- 1 tablespoon finely chopped fresh parsley
- 1 tablespoon finely chopped fresh rosemary
- 2 teaspoons finely chopped fresh thyme
- 1 clove garlic, finely chopped
- 1 teaspoon crushed black peppercorns
- Finely grated zest and freshly squeezed juice of 1 unwaxed lemon
- 1 teaspoon red chile paste
- 4 tablespoons (60 ml) extra-virgin olive oil
- 4 boneless skinless chicken breast halves, cut in small cubes
- Lemon wedges, to serve

Mix the parsley, rosemary, thyme, garlic, black pepper, lemon zest and juice, chile paste, and 2 tablespoons of oil in a medium bowl. Add the chicken and toss well. Marinate for at least 10 minutes.

Preheat a grill pan or barbecue on high. Thread the chicken onto skewers. Cook on the grill, turning and brushing often with the remaining 2 tablespoons of oil, until tender and golden, about 10 minutes. Serve hot with lemon wedges.

SERVES 4 • PREPARATION 10 MIN. + 10 MIN. TO MARINATE • COOKING 10 MIN. • LEVEL 1

2 chicken kebabs
with soy & cilantro

- 2 cups (400 g) jasmine rice
- 2 tablespoons Thai sweet chile sauce
- 2 tablespoons freshly squeezed lime juice
- 1 tablespoon light soy sauce
- 1 tablespoon finely chopped fresh cilantro (coriander)
- 3 boneless skinless chicken breast halves, sliced

Bring a large saucepan of salted water to a boil. Add the rice and cook over medium heat until tender, 10–15 minutes. Drain well.

Mix the sweet chile sauce, lime juice, soy sauce, and cilantro in a small bowl. Add the chicken and coat well.

Preheat a grill pan or barbecue on high. Thread the chicken onto skewers. Grill until tender and golden, about 10 minutes. Serve the kebabs hot with the rice.

SERVES 4 • PREPARATION 15 MIN. • COOKING 15 MIN. • LEVEL 1

3 chicken
with lemon & caper sauce

- 4 boneless skinless chicken breast halves
- 1 cup (150 g) all-purpose (plain) flour, seasoned with salt and freshly ground pepper
- 6 tablespoons (90 g) butter
- 1 tablespoon capers, drained
- 1 tablespoon finely grated unwaxed lemon zest
- 5 tablespoons (75 ml) freshly squeezed lemon juice
- Salt and freshly ground black pepper
- Boiled new potatoes and salad greens, to serve

Dredge the chicken in the seasoned flour until well coated. Shake off any excess.

Heat 2 tablespoons of butter in a large frying pan over medium heat. Add the chicken and sauté until tender and golden, 6–8 minutes each side. Transfer to serving dishes and keep warm.

Add the remaining 4 tablespoons of butter, capers, and lemon zest and juice to the pan. Simmer over low heat, stirring often, until thickened, about 5 minutes. Season with salt and pepper.

Spoon the sauce over the chicken. Serve hot with the potatoes and salad greens.

SERVES 4 • PREPARATION 10 MIN. • COOKING 20 MIN. • LEVEL 1

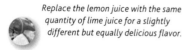

Replace the lemon juice with the same quantity of lime juice for a slightly different but equally delicious flavor.

4 grilled chicken
with figs & feta cheese

- 4 boneless skinless chicken breast halves
- 4 fresh figs, cut in half lengthwise
- 2 tablespoons extra-virgin olive oil
- Salt and freshly ground black pepper
- 5 ounces (150 g) feta cheese, cubed
- 3 cups (150 g) arugula (rocket) leaves
- Finely shredded zest and juice of 1 unwaxed orange

Preheat a grill pan or barbecue on high. Brush the chicken and figs with the oil. Season with salt and pepper. Grill the chicken until golden and cooked through, 5–6 minutes on each side. Grill the figs for 2–3 minutes on each side until slightly softened.

Toss the feta, arugula, and orange zest and juice in a medium bowl. Add the figs to the bowl and toss gently. Thinly slice the chicken and add to the bowl. Serve hot.

SERVES 4 • PREPARATION 10 MIN. • COOKING 10–12 MIN. • LEVEL 1

5 grilled chicken
with lemon, garlic & tomatoes

- ¼ cup (60 ml) extra-virgin olive oil
- Finely grated zest and juice of 1 unwaxed lemon
- 2 cloves garlic, finely chopped
- 2 tablespoons finely chopped fresh parsley
- 4 boneless skinless chicken breast halves, halved lengthwise
- Salt and freshly ground black pepper
- 2 cups (100 g) arugula (rocket) leaves
- 4 tomatoes, cut into wedges

Mix the oil, lemon zest and juice, garlic, and parsley in a small dish. Add the chicken and coat well. Season with salt and pepper.

Preheat a grill pan or barbecue on high. Grill the chicken until golden and cooked through, 5–6 minutes on each side. Serve hot with the arugula and tomatoes.

SERVES **4** • PREPARATION **10** MIN. • COOKING **10–12** MIN. • LEVEL **1**

6 duck yakitori
with scallions

Yakitori Sauce
- 1/2 cup (120 ml) soy sauce
- 1/3 cup (90 ml) chicken stock
- 1/4 cup (60 ml) mirin
- 1/4 cup (50 g) superfine (caster) sugar

Skewers
- 1 3/4 pounds (800 g) boneless duck breasts, trimmed and cut into 1-inch (2.5-cm) pieces
- 8 scallions (spring onions), trimmed and cut into 2-inch (5-cm) lengths
- Steamed long-grain rice, to serve

Yakitori Sauce Combine the soy sauce, stock, mirin, and sugar in a small saucepan. Bring to a boil, stirring from time to time, over high heat. Reduce the heat and simmer until the sauce is reduced by about one-third, about 5 minutes. Set aside to cool slightly. Pour into a shallow ceramic dish.

Skewers Divide the ingredients evenly, and thread the duck and scallions (crosswise) onto the skewers. Place the skewers in the yakitori sauce. Turn to coat in the sauce.

Preheat a grill pan or barbecue on high. Grill the skewers, basting with the yakitori sauce from time to time, until just cooked through, 8–10 minutes. Serve hot with the rice.

SERVES 4 • PREPARATION 10 MIN. • COOKING 8–10 MIN. • LEVEL 1

Yakitori is a Japanese term that means grilled (yaki) fowl (tori). The meat is usually cooked on skewers. Try this sauce with chicken or turkey too. If using bamboo skewers, presoak them in cold water for 30 minutes before grilling. Mirin is a sweet Japanese wine made from rice. It is rather like sake, but has a lower alcohol content.

7 crumbed turkey
with sweet potato mash

- 1½ cups (120 g) fresh bread crumbs
- ¼ cup finely chopped fresh sage leaves
- Salt and freshly ground black pepper
- 4 turkey breast fillets, about 5 ounces (150 g) each
- 2 tablespoons all-purpose (plain) flour
- 2 large eggs, lightly beaten
- 1¾ pounds (800 g) sweet potatoes, peeled and cut into large chunks
- ⅓ cup (90 ml) milk, hot
- 2 tablespoons butter, diced
- Pinch of ground nutmeg
- 2 tablespoons extra-virgin olive oil

Combine the bread crumbs and sage in a shallow dish. Season with salt and pepper. Coat the turkey with the flour and eggs then press into the crumb mixture.

Boil the sweet potatoes until tender, about 10 minutes. Drain and return to the pan. Add the milk, butter, nutmeg, salt, and pepper. Mash until smooth.

Heat the oil in a frying pan over medium heat. Cook the turkey until golden and crisp, 3–4 minutes each side. Serve hot with the sweet potatoes.

SERVES 4 • PREPARATION 15 MIN. • COOKING 10 MIN. • LEVEL 1

8 sautéed turkey
with marmalade glaze

- 1 tablespoon extra-virgin olive oil
- 3 tablespoons butter
- 8 turkey cutlets (about 1½ pounds/750 g)
- ½ cup (150 ml) orange marmalade
- 3 tablespoons freshly squeezed orange juice
- ¼ cup (60 ml) chicken stock
- Salt and freshly ground black pepper
- 2 bunches asparagus, trimmed

Heat the oil and butter in a large frying pan over medium heat. Sauté the turkey until golden and cooked, 5–8 minutes. Transfer to a plate and keep warm.

Add the marmalade, orange juice, and chicken stock to the pan. Season with salt and pepper. Simmer over medium heat until slightly thickened, about 5 minutes.

Steam the asparagus until just tender, 2–4 minutes. Arrange the asparagus and turkey on serving plates. Spoon the marmalade glaze over the top and serve hot.

SERVES 4 • PREPARATION 10 MIN. • COOKING 15 MIN. • LEVEL 1

9 veal escalopes
with pizza topping

- 1¼ pounds (600 g) small, thinly sliced veal escalopes (cut from the rump)
- 1 cup (150 g) all-purpose (plain) flour
- 4 tablespoons (60 ml) extra-virgin olive oil
- Salt and freshly ground black pepper
- 2 cloves garlic, finely chopped
- 2 tablespoons finely chopped parsley + extra to sprinkle
- 1 pound (500 g) tomatoes, peeled and finely chopped
- 1 tablespoon capers
- 4 ounces (120 g) mozzarella cheese, thinly sliced
- Pinch of hot chile powder, to dust

Lightly pound the escalopes with a meat tenderizer so that they are thin and of even thickness. Dredge in the flour, shaking off any excess.

Heat 2 tablespoons of oil in a large frying pan over high heat. Add the escalopes and brown on both sides, about 5 minutes (depending on the thickness of the meat). Season with salt and pepper. Remove and set aside, keeping warm.

Heat the remaining 2 tablespoons of oil in the same pan. Add the garlic and parsley and sauté for 2–3 minutes. Add the tomatoes and capers and simmer until reduced, about 8–10 minutes. Return the veal to the pan, spooning the sauce over the top.

Top each escalope with a slice of mozzarella and season with salt and pepper. Simmer for 5 minutes, until the mozzarella has melted a little.

Sprinkle with the extra parsley, dust with the chile powder, and serve hot.

SERVES **4** • PREPARATION **10** MIN. • COOKING **20** MIN. • LEVEL **1**

Escalopes, also known as scallops or scaloppine, are thin slices of veal (or other meat) that have been lightly pounded to thin them down for quick cooking.

10 veal escalopes
with arugula, parmesan & balsamic vinegar

- 1¼ pounds (600 g) small, thinly sliced veal escalopes (cut from the rump)
- Salt and freshly ground black pepper
- 2 tablespoons extra-virgin olive oil
- 3 tablespoons balsamic vinegar
- 2 cups (100 g) arugula (rocket), coarsely chopped
- 5 ounces (150 g) Parmesan cheese, shaved

Lightly pound the veal with a meat tenderizer so that it is thin and of even thickness. Season the veal with salt and pepper.

Heat the oil in a large frying pan over high heat. Add the escalopes and brown on both sides, about 5 minutes (depending on the thickness of the meat). Add the balsamic vinegar and let it evaporate. Add the arugula and let it wilt for 1 minute.

Remove from the heat and let rest for 3 minutes. Sprinkle with the Parmesan and season with salt and pepper. Serve hot.

SERVES 4 • PREPARATION 10 MIN. • COOKING 10 MIN. • LEVEL 1

11 veal escalopes
with tomatoes, eggplant & cheese

- 1¼ pounds (600 g) small, thinly sliced veal escalopes (cut from the rump)
- 2 tablespoons butter
- 5 tablespoons (75 ml) extra-virgin olive oil
- 4 slices mozzarella cheese
- 4 tomatoes, cut in half
- 1 large eggplant (aubergine), thinly sliced
- 1 cup (250 ml) beef stock
- 4 sprigs fresh thyme

Lightly pound the veal with a meat tenderizer. Heat the butter and 3 tablespoons of oil in a large frying pan over high heat. Add the escalopes and brown on both sides, about 5 minutes.

Preheat an overhead broiler (grill). Place a slice of mozzarella on each escalope. Broil until melted, about 2 minutes. Brush the tomatoes and eggplant with the remaining 2 tablespoons of oil and broil until tender, about 5 minutes. Top each escalope with 2 slices of eggplant and half a tomato. Heat the pan juices with the stock and thyme. Pour over the veal and serve hot.

SERVES 4 • PREPARATION 10 MIN. • COOKING 15 MIN. • LEVEL 1

12 veal escalopes
with lemon

- 1¹/₄ pounds (600 g) small, thinly sliced veal escalopes (cut from the rump)
- Salt and freshly ground black pepper
- ¹/₂ cup (75 g) all-purpose (plain) flour
- 2¹/₂ tablespoons butter
- 2 tablespoons extra-virgin olive oil
- ¹/₂ cup (120 ml) beef stock
- Freshly squeezed juice of 1 lemon
- 1 tablespoon finely chopped fresh parsley
- Fresh salad greens, to serve

Lightly pound the veal with a meat tenderizer so that it is thin and of even thickness. Season the veal with salt and pepper. Dredge the escalopes in the flour, shaking off any excess.

Heat the butter and oil in a large frying pan over high heat. Add the escalopes and lightly brown on both sides, 2–3 minutes. Lower the heat to medium and continue cooking, adding a little stock to moisten. After 7–10 minutes, when the veal is cooked to your liking, turn off the heat. Drizzle with the lemon juice.

Sprinkle with the parsley and serve hot with the salad greens.

SERVES 4 • PREPARATION 10 MIN. • COOKING 12–15 MIN. • LEVEL 1

You can vary this recipe by replacing the lemon juice with freshly squeezed orange juice, or by sprinkling the cooked meat with a few shavings of Parmesan cheese.

13 chicken & broccoli stir-fry

- 3 tablespoons peanut oil
- 1/2 cup (80 g) cashew nuts
- 1 3/4 pounds (800 g) boneless skinless chicken thighs
- 1 onion, cut into thin wedges
- 1 head broccoli, broken into florets
- 3 cloves garlic, finely chopped
- 1/2 cup (120 ml) Chinese oyster sauce
- 3 tablespoons soy sauce
- Steamed jasmine rice, to serve

Heat 1 tablespoon of oil in a wok over high heat. Add the cashews and stir-fry until golden, 2–3 minutes. Transfer to a plate. Heat 1 tablespoon of oil in the same wok over high heat. Stir-fry half the chicken until golden and almost cooked through, 3–4 minutes. Transfer to a plate. Repeat with the remaining chicken.

Heat the remaining 1 tablespoon of oil in the wok. Add the onion and stir-fry until tender, about 2 minutes. Add the broccoli and garlic. Stir-fry until bright green, about 2 minutes. Add the oyster sauce, soy sauce, and chicken to the wok. Stir-fry until hot. Add the cashews and toss well. Serve hot with the rice.

SERVES 4 • PREPARATION 15 MIN. • COOKING 15 MIN. • LEVEL 1

14 thai beef stir-fry

- 1½ cups (300 g) jasmine rice
- 2 cups (500 ml) canned coconut milk
- ¾ cup (180 ml) water
- ½ teaspoon salt
- 2 tablespoons Asian fish sauce
- 2 tablespoons soy sauce
- 1 teaspoon sugar
- 1 tablespoon vegetable oil
- 3 cloves garlic, sliced
- 3 long red chiles, seeded and sliced into 2-inch (5-cm) matchsticks
- 1¼ pounds (600 g) ground (minced) beef sirloin
- 1 cup (50 g) torn fresh basil leaves

Rinse the rice under cold running water until the water runs clear. Combine the rice, coconut milk, water, and salt in a medium saucepan. Bring to a boil over high heat. Decrease the heat to low, cover, and simmer until tender and the liquid is absorbed, 12–15 minutes.

Combine the fish sauce, soy sauce, and sugar in a small bowl. Heat the oil in a wok over high heat. Add the garlic and half the chiles. Stir-fry for 15 seconds. Add the beef and stir-fry until browned, about 4 minutes. Pour in the soy mixture and stir-fry for 30 seconds. Add the remaining chiles and the basil and stir to combine. Serve hot over the coconut rice.

SERVES **4** • PREPARATION **10** MIN. • COOKING **20** MIN. • LEVEL **1**

15 pork escalopes
with marsala wine

- 2 tablespoons butter
- 2 tablespoons extra-virgin olive oil
- 2 cloves garlic, crushed but whole
- 8 thin escalopes (slices) pork loin, about 1½ pounds (600 g) total weight
- Salt and freshly ground black pepper
- ½ cup (120 ml) dry Marsala wine
- 1 teaspoon cornstarch (cornflour) flour

Heat 1 tablespoon of butter with the oil in a large frying pan over medium heat. Add the garlic and sauté until pale golden brown. Remove and discard the garlic.

Add the pork and season with salt and pepper. Cook until tender on one side, 2–3 minutes, then turn and cook the other side. Remove the escalopes from the pan and set aside on a serving dish in a warm oven.

Add the Marsala, remaining 1 tablespoon of butter, and cornstarch to the pan and simmer over low heat until thickened. Pour the sauce over the pork and serve hot.

SERVES 4 • PREPARATION 15 MIN. • COOKING 15 MIN. • LEVEL 1

Marsala is a fortified wine produced near the town of Marsala in western Sicily. It is widely used in cooking, especially in Italy and the United States. Replace with dry sherry if preferred.

16 grilled pork
with bean salad

- 1 (14-ounce/400-g) can cannellini beans, drained
- 2 tomatoes, diced
- 4 ounces (120 g) feta cheese, crumbled
- 1 tablespoon dried oregano
- 2 tablespoons extra-virgin olive oil
- Salt and freshly ground black pepper
- 4 pork loin steaks
- 1 lemon, cut into wedges, to serve
- Tzatziki (see page 204), to serve

Mix the beans, tomatoes, feta, oregano, and 1 tablespoon of oil in a large bowl. Season with salt and pepper.

Preheat a grill pan or barbecue on high. Drizzle the pork with the remaining 1 tablespoon of oil. Season with salt and pepper. Grill the pork until cooked, 4–5 minutes each side. Arrange on serving plates. Top with the bean salad. Serve hot with the lemon wedges and tzatziki.

SERVES **4–6** • PREPARATION **15** MIN. • COOKING **8–10** MIN. • LEVEL **1**

17 grilled pork
with sage & lemon

- 8–12 leaves fresh sage
- 2 tablespoons extra-virgin olive oil
- 4 pork loin steaks
- 2 tablespoons butter
- 2 cloves garlic, finely chopped
- 1/4 cup (60 ml) chicken stock
- 1 pound (500 g) asparagus, trimmed
- Finely grated zest and juice of 1 unwaxed lemon
- Salt and freshly ground black pepper

Sauté the sage in the oil in a large frying pan over medium-high heat until crisp, about 2 minutes. Remove from the pan and drain on paper towels. Sauté the pork in the sage-flavored oil until cooked, 4–5 minutes on each side. Set the pork aside in a warm oven.

Add the butter, garlic, chicken stock, and asparagus to the pan. Bring to a boil then simmer until the asparagus is tender, about 3 minutes. Stir in the lemon juice. Season with salt and pepper. Transfer the asparagus to serving plates. Top with the pork and drizzle with the pan juices. Garnish with the lemon zest and sage. Serve hot.

SERVES 4–6 • PREPARATION 10 MIN. • COOKING 15 MIN. • LEVEL 1

18 parmesan veal rolls

- 8 tablespoons (120 g) butter
- 2 tablespoons finely chopped fresh parsley
- 2 cloves garlic, finely chopped
- 1 cup (150 g) fine dry bread crumbs
- 1¼ cups (150 g) freshly grated Parmesan cheese
- 2 large eggs, lightly beaten
- Salt and freshly ground black pepper
- 12 small thin veal escalopes
- 1 small onion, finely chopped
- 2 tablespoons tomato paste (concentrate) diluted in ½ cup (120 ml) water

Melt 4 tablespoons (60 g) of the butter in a small saucepan over low heat. Add the parsley, garlic, bread crumbs, Parmesan, eggs, salt, and pepper and mix well.

Lay the veal out on a clean work surface. Spread the bread crumb mixture on each slice of the veal. Roll up and secure with toothpicks.

Heat the remaining 4 tablespoons (60 g) of butter in a large frying pan over medium heat. Sauté the onion until softened, 3–4 minutes. Add the diluted tomato paste and season with salt and pepper.

Place the veal rolls in the pan in a single layer. Cover and simmer over low heat, turning frequently, until the meat is tender and cooked through, about 10 minutes. Serve hot.

SERVES 4–6 • PREPARATION 15 MIN. • COOKING 15 MIN. • LEVEL 2

Serve these delicious veal rolls with rice, potatoes, or freshly baked bread to soak up the tomato sauce.

19 roasted chicken rolls
with cheese

- 4 boneless skinless chicken breast fillets
- 5 ounces (150 g) Gruyère cheese, thinly sliced
- 2 tablespoons finely chopped fresh chives
- 1 tablespoon extra-virgin olive oil
- 1/3 cup (90 g) butter
- 1 bunch spinach, trimmed
- Salt and freshly ground black pepper
- Pinch ground nutmeg

Preheat the oven to 400°F (200°C/gas 6). Line a baking sheet with parchment paper. Make a slit lengthwise through each chicken breast to form a pocket (do not cut all the way through). Stuff the cheese and chives inside each pocket.

Heat the oil in a large frying pan over medium-high heat. Sauté the chicken in batches until golden, about 2 minutes each side. Transfer the chicken to the baking sheet. Roast for 6–8 minutes, until just cooked through. Cover and let rest for 5 minutes.

Heat the butter in the frying pan over medium heat. Sauté the spinach until just wilted, 2–3 minutes. Season with salt, pepper, and the nutmeg. Slice the chicken and serve hot with the spinach.

SERVES 4 • PREPARATION 15 MIN. • COOKING 15 MIN. • LEVEL 2

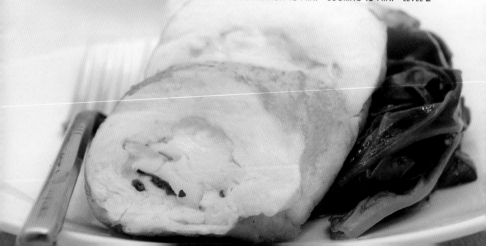

20 chicken rolls
with pancetta & parmesan

- 2 cups (400 g) short-grain rice
- 2 boneless skinless chicken breasts, cut into 8 fillets
- 8 slices pancetta or bacon
- 3 ounces (90 g) Parmesan cheese, cut into small cubes
- 16 leaves fresh sage
- 1/4 teaspoon freshly grated nutmeg
- 1/4 cup (60 ml) extra-virgin olive oil
- 1/3 cup (90 ml) dry white wine

Cook the rice in a large pan of salted boiling water until tender, about 15 minutes. Drain and rinse well.

Lay the chicken out on a clean work surface. Place a slice of pancetta, some Parmesan, and two sage leaves on top of each chicken fillet. Season with the nutmeg. Roll up the slices and secure with toothpicks.

Heat the oil in a large frying pan over high heat. Add the chicken and sauté until lightly browned, about 3 minutes. Drizzle with the wine. Cook over medium-low heat, turning often, until cooked and golden, 10–12 minutes. Serve hot with the rice.

SERVES 4 • PREPARATION 15 MIN. • COOKING 15 MIN. • LEVEL 2

1

baked chicken
with apricots & rice

2

baked pork
with apples & mash

3

peppered steak
with arugula

4

balsamic steak
with caramelized onions

5

grilled steak
with tomato salad

TOP
20

6

veal roll with
prosciutto & cheese filling

7

honey-roasted lamb
with parsnip mash

8

lamb cutlets
with halloumi

9

breaded lamb chops

10

chicken kebabs
cajun-style

11

lamb koftas
with minted couscous

12

calf liver
with marsala & mash

13

teriyaki chicken

14

chinese pork spareribs

just a few
ingredients

15

veal & cream casserole

16

coconut lamb
with rice

17

beef vindaloo
with rice

18

veal escalopes
with parmesan cheese

19

orange-glazed chicken
with couscous

20

balsamic chicken
with roasted tomatoes

1 baked chicken
with apricots & rice

- 1 (14-ounce/400-g) can apricot halves, with half the juice reserved
- 1 cup (250 ml) chicken stock
- 1 tablespoon apple cider vinegar
- 4 boneless skinless chicken breast halves
- 1½ cups (300 g) basmati rice

Preheat the oven to 375°F (190°C/gas 5). Combine the apricots and juice, chicken stock, and apple cider vinegar in a medium saucepan and bring to a boil.

Arrange the chicken breasts in a baking dish in a single layer and pour in the apricot mixture. Bake for 10 minutes. Remove from the oven and baste with the juices. Bake for 15 minutes, basting every 5 minutes.

Bring a large saucepan of salted water to a boil. Add the rice and cook until tender, 10–15 minutes. Drain well. Arrange the rice on serving plates, topped with the chicken and sauce. Serve hot.

SERVES 4 • PREPARATION 10 MIN. • COOKING 25–30 MIN. • LEVEL 1

2 baked pork
with apples & mash

- 6 Golden Delicious apples, halved and cored
- 2 cups (500 ml) dry white wine
- 2 pork fillets, about 1 pound (500 g)
- Salt and freshly ground black pepper
- ¼ cup (60 ml) extra-virgin olive oil
- Garlic mash (see page 285), to serve

Place the apples in a bowl, cover with the wine, and set aside to marinate for at least 2 hours.

Preheat the oven to 400°F (200°C/gas 6). Drain the pork, reserving the marinade. Season the pork with salt and pepper and place in a baking pan with the oil. Bake for 10 minutes, then drizzle with half the marinade. Turn the pork and bake for 20 minutes.

Arrange the apples around the pork in the pan. Add more wine if the pan is dry. Bake for 30 minutes, until cooked through. Slice and transfer to a serving dish. Serve hot with the garlic mash.

SERVES 4 • PREPARATION 10 MIN. + 2 HR. TO MARINATE • COOKING 1 HR. • LEVEL 1

3 peppered steak
with arugula

- 1^1/$_2$ pounds (750 g) sirloin or tenderloin steak, boned
- Salt
- 2–3 tablespoons whole black pepper corns
- 4 tablespoons (60 ml) extra-virgin olive oil
- 2–3 cups (100–150 g) baby arugula (rocket) leaves

Put the steak on a work surface and season generously with salt. Put the whole black peppercorns on a work surface and cover with foil. Use a meat tenderizer to smash the pepper, so that the corns are cracked. Sprinkle over the meat, working it into the surface with your fingertips.

Preheat a grill pan or barbecue on high. Drizzle with 1 tablespoon of oil. Cook the steak on the grill until browned on the outside and cooked to your liking within, 5–10 minutes, depending on how thick the steak is and how well done you like it. Transfer to a serving platter or board.

Put the arugula in a bowl, season with salt, and drizzle with the remaining 3 tablespoons of oil. Toss well to coat. Slice the steak and serve hot with the arugula.

SERVES 4 • PREPARATION 15 MIN. • COOKING 5–10 MIN. • LEVEL 1

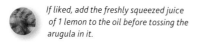

If liked, add the freshly squeezed juice of 1 lemon to the oil before tossing the arugula in it.

4 balsamic steak
with caramelized onions

- 4 tablespoons (60 ml) extra-virgin olive oil
- 6 onions, thinly sliced
- 3/4 cup (180 ml) balsamic vinegar
- 4 thick beef filet mignon (fillet/eye fillet) steaks, about 6 ounces (180 g) each
- 2 cups (100 g) arugula (rocket) leaves

Heat 2 tablespoons of oil in a large frying pan over low heat. Add the onions and simmer until caramelized, about 30 minutes. Heat the balsamic vinegar in a small saucepan over medium heat until it reduces by half.

Heat the remaining 2 tablespoons of oil in a large frying pan over medium-high heat. Cook the steaks for 3–4 minutes on each side. Remove from the heat. Cover and let rest for 5 minutes.

Serve the steaks on individual plates, topped with the onions and balsamic sauce with the arugula on the side.

SERVES 4 • PREPARATION 15 MIN. • COOKING 30 MIN. • LEVEL 1

5 grilled steak
with tomato salad

- 4 beef filet mignon (fillet/eye fillet) steaks, about 6 ounces (180 g) each
- 3/4 cup (180 ml) smoky barbecue sauce
- 6 tomatoes, thinly sliced
- 1 red onion, thinly sliced
- 1/2 cup (50 g) black olives

Put the beef in a large bowl and cover with the smoky barbecue sauce. Cover and refrigerate for 1 hour.

Preheat a grill pan or barbecue on high. Cook the steaks for 5–10 minutes each, depending on how well done you like your steak. Remove from the heat. Cover and let rest for 5 minutes.

Serve the steaks hot on individual plates, topped with the tomatoes, onion, and olives.

SERVES 4 • PREPARATION 10 MIN. + 1 HR. TO MARINATE • COOKING 5–10 MIN. • LEVEL 1

6 veal roll
with cheese & prosciutto filling

- 1 large slice veal, cut from the rump, about 1½ pounds (750 g)
- Salt and freshly ground black pepper
- 4 ounces (120 g) prosciutto
- 6 ounces (180 g) Fontina or mozzarella cheese, sliced
- ¼ cup (60 ml) extra-virgin olive oil
- 2 cups (500 ml) milk

Cut off any small pieces of fat from the meat. Cover with foil (to prevent the meat from breaking) and pound lightly with a meat tenderizer to make a large thin slice.

Season with salt and pepper and cover with slices of prosciutto and cheese. Roll the veal up tightly (with the grain of the meat running parallel to the length of the roll, so that it will be easier to slice) and tie firmly with kitchen string.

Heat the oil over medium-low heat in a heavy-bottomed saucepan just large enough to contain the roll. Brown the roll on all sides, about 10 minutes. Season with salt and pepper. Pour in the milk (which should cover the roll), partially cover the saucepan, and simmer over medium heat until the milk reduces. This will take about 50 minutes. Turn the meat from time to time during cooking.

Transfer to a serving dish, slice, and serve hot with the sauce from the pan.

SERVES 4 • PREPARATION 15 MIN. • COOKING 1 HR. • LEVEL 2

This roll can be prepared ahead of time and be either reheated or served at room temperature. If serving cold, reheat the sauce before drizzling over the sliced roll. If liked, serve with fresh salad greens and boiled potatoes or rice.

7 honey-roasted lamb
with parsnip mash

- 1 (3-pound/1.5-kg) rack of lamb
- ½ cup (125 ml) honey mustard
- ⅓ cup (90 ml) extra-virgin olive oil
- 8–10 parsnips, peeled and diced
- ½ cup (120 ml) crème fraîche

Put the lamb in a large bowl. Smear with the honey mustard and oil. Cover with plastic wrap (cling film) and marinate in the refrigerator for 1 hour.

Preheat the oven to 350°F (180°C/gas 4). Arrange the lamb in a single layer in a large baking dish. Bake for 25–30 minutes, until tender. Let rest for 10 minutes.

Cook the parsnips in a large pot of boiling water until tender, 8–10 minutes. Drain well and return to the pan. Add the crème fraîche and mash until smooth.

Slice the lamb and serve hot with the mashed parsnip.

SERVES **4** • PREPARATION **20** MIN. + **1** HR. TO MARINATE • COOKING **30–40** MIN. • LEVEL **1**

8 lamb cutlets
with halloumi

- 12 lamb cutlets, cut about ½ inch (1.5 cm) thick
- 3 tablespoons extra-virgin olive oil
- Finely grated zest and juice of 2 unwaxed lemons
- 8 ounces (250 g) halloumi cheese, thickly sliced
- 3 cups (150 g) arugula (rocket) leaves

Put the lamb in a large bowl with 1 tablespoon of oil and the zest and juice of 1 lemon. Cover and chill for 1 hour.

Drain the lamb and fry in a large nonstick frying pan over medium-high heat until cooked, 4–5 minutes on each side. Remove from the pan and set aside. Fry the cheese in 1 tablespoon of oil over high heat until browned, 2 minutes on each side. Drain on paper towels.

Mix the arugula, fried halloumi, remaining 1 tablespoon of oil, and remaining lemon zest and juice in a medium bowl. Toss well. Arrange the salad on individual serving plates and top with the lamb cutlets. Serve hot.

SERVES 4 • PREPARATION 10 MIN. + 1 HR. TO MARINATE • COOKING 12–15 MIN. • LEVEL 1

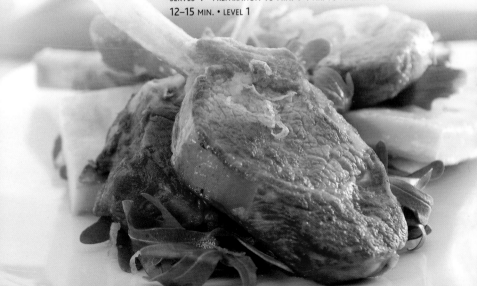

9 breaded lamb chops

- 8 lamb chops, cut from the rib
- Salt
- ½ cup (75 g) all-purpose (plain) flour
- 2 large eggs, lightly beaten
- 1 cup (150 g) fine dry bread crumbs
- 1 cup (250 ml) olive oil, for frying

Lightly pound the chops with a meat tenderizer to spread the meat as much as possible.

Sprinkle with salt, and dredge in the flour, shaking to remove excess. Dip in the egg, then coat well in the bread crumbs.

Heat the oil in a heavy-bottomed pan to 365°F (185°C). If you don't have a frying thermometer, test the oil temperature by dropping a small piece of bread into the hot oil. If the bread immediately bubbles to the surface and turns golden the oil is ready.

Fry the chops, turning often, until golden brown on both sides and cooked through, 5–10 minutes, depending on the thickness of the chops.

Drain on paper towels and serve very hot.

SERVES 4 • PREPARATION 10 MIN. • COOKING 5–10 MIN. • LEVEL 1

Many people enjoy the distinctive flavor of lamb and mutton while others find it too strong. Remember that the flavor increases as the sheep ages, so if you want tender meat with a more refined taste, buy young lamb.

10 chicken kebabs
cajun-style

- 3 tablespoons extra-virgin olive oil
- 2 tablespoons Cajun spice mix
- 6 boneless skinless chicken breast halves, cut into small pieces
- 1½ cups (300 g) long-grain rice
- 1 (14-ounce/400-g) can kidney beans, drained

Mix the oil and Cajun spice mix in a large bowl. Coat the chicken with the mixture. Cover with plastic wrap (cling film) and marinate in the refrigerator for 1 hour. Thread the chicken onto metal skewers and set aside.

Bring a large saucepan of salted water to a boil. Add the rice and cook over medium heat for 12 minutes. Add the kidney beans and cook for 3 minutes until the rice is tender. Drain well.

Preheat a grill pan or barbecue on high. Grill the kebabs until cooked through, 10–15 minutes. Serve hot with the rice and kidney beans.

SERVES **4–6** • PREPARATION **15** MIN. **+ 1** HR. TO MARINATE • COOKING **20–30** MIN. • LEVEL **1**

11 lamb koftas
with minted couscous

- 1½ pounds (750 g) ground (minced) lamb
- 1 red bell pepper (capsicum), seeded and finely chopped
- 2 cups (400 g) instant couscous
- 3 tablespoons finely chopped fresh mint
- 2 cups (500 ml) chicken stock, hot

Combine the lamb and bell pepper in a food processor and process until a coarse paste forms. Use wet hands to shape the mixture into twelve sausage-shaped lengths. Thread each kofta onto a metal skewer.

Mix the couscous and mint in a medium bowl. Pour the stock over the couscous mixture. Cover the bowl and let stand until the couscous has absorbed the liquid, about 10 minutes. Fluff up with a fork and set aside.

Preheat a grill pan or barbecue on high. Grill the koftas until cooked through, about 5 minutes on each side. Serve hot on a bed of the minted couscous.

SERVES 4 • PREPARATION 15 MIN. • COOKING 10 MIN. • LEVEL 1

12 calf liver
with marsala & mash

- 1 pound (500 g) calf liver, thinly sliced
- Salt and freshly ground black pepper
- ½ cup (75 g) all-purpose (plain) flour
- ⅓ cup (90 g) butter
- ⅓ cup (90 ml) dry Marsala wine
- Mashed potatoes, to serve

Season the calf liver with salt and pepper and dredge in the flour, shaking off any excess.

Melt the butter in a large frying pan over medium-high heat. Add the calf liver and cook on one side until tender, 2–3 minutes. Turn and add the Marsala. Cook until tender, 2–3 minutes.

Transfer to a heated serving dish. Serve hot with the mashed potatoes.

SERVES **4** · PREPARATION **10** MIN. · COOKING **5–10** MIN. · LEVEL **1**

Calf liver is a highly nutritious food. It is an excellent source of protein, vitamin A, many of the B vitamins, and many minerals. It also contains a lot of cholesterol so should not be eaten every day.

13 teriyaki chicken

- 20 chicken wings
- 3/4 cup (180 ml) teriyaki sauce
- 6 tomatoes, coarsely chopped
- 3 tablespoons fresh cilantro (coriander) leaves
- 1 1/2 cups (300 g) basmati rice

Put the chicken wings in a large bowl and cover with the teriyaki sauce. Cover with plastic wrap (cling film) and refrigerate for 1 hour.

Combine the tomatoes and cilantro in a medium bowl and mix well. Bring a large saucepan of salted water to a boil. Add the rice and cook over medium heat until tender, 10–15 minutes. Drain well and keep warm.

Preheat a grill pan or barbecue on high. Grill the chicken until cooked through, about 5 minutes on each side. Serve hot with the tomatoes and rice.

SERVES 4 • PREPARATION 10 MIN. + 1 HR. TO MARINATE • COOKING 20–25 MIN. • LEVEL 1

14 chinese pork spareribs

- 12 pork spareribs
- ⅔ cup (150 ml) Chinese plum sauce
- 1½ cups (300 g) wild rice
- 3 tablespoons Asian sesame oil
- 3 tablespoons fresh cilantro (coriander) leaves

Place the spareribs in a large bowl and cover with the plum sauce. Cover with plastic wrap (cling film) and refrigerate for 1 hour.

Bring a large saucepan of salted water to a boil. Add the rice and cook over medium heat for 10–15 minutes, until tender. Drain well and set aside.

Place a grill pan over medium-high heat. Brush the grill with the sesame oil. Grill the spareribs for 5–6 minutes on each side, until cooked through. Arrange the rice on serving plates and top with the spareribs. Garnish with the cilantro and serve hot.

SERVES 4 • PREPARATION 5 MIN. + 1 HR. TO MARINATE • COOKING 20–30 MIN. • LEVEL 1

15 veal & cream casserole

- 1¼ pounds (600 g) veal, shank or shoulder, cut into 1¼-inch (3-cm) cubes
- Salt and freshly ground white pepper
- 4 tablespoons (60 g) butter
- 1–2 tablespoons all-purpose (plain) flour
- 1½ cups (370 ml) light (single) cream + extra, as required
- Freshly cooked rice, to serve

Season the meat with salt and pepper. Heat 1 tablespoon of butter in a heavy-bottomed saucepan over medium heat until it stops foaming. Add the veal and brown, stirring frequently, 10–15 minutes.

While the meat is browning, melt the remaining 3 tablespoons of butter in a small saucepan. Add the flour and stir with a wooden spoon over medium heat until it starts to color, 2–3 minutes. Add the flour mixture to the meat and simmer for a few minutes, stirring continuously.

Stir in the cream. Cover and simmer over low heat until the meat is very tender, at least 1 hour. Stir often during cooking. If the liquid reduces too much, add 1–2 tablespoons extra of cream or water. There should be plenty of sauce.

Check the seasoning and serve hot with the rice.

SERVES 4 · PREPARATION 15 MIN. · COOKING 1½ HR. · LEVEL 1

You can add a little extra color and flavor to this dish by sprinkling each portion with coarsely chopped fresh parsley just before serving.

16 coconut lamb
with rice

- 1³/₄ pounds (800 g) lamb fillet (tenderloin), diced
- 6 tomatoes, coarsely chopped
- 1–2 teaspoons curry powder
- 2 cups (500 ml) coconut milk
- Salt and freshly ground white pepper
- 1¹/₂ cups (300 g) basmati rice

Cook the lamb with the tomatoes and curry powder in a large frying pan over medium heat for 2 minutes. Pour in the coconut milk and season with salt and pepper. Cover and simmer over low heat until the lamb is tender, 35–40 minutes.

Bring a large saucepan of salted water to a boil. Add the rice and cook over medium heat until tender, 10–15 minutes. Drain well.

Serve the lamb and its sauce hot on a bed of the rice.

SERVES 4 · PREPARATION 10 MIN. · COOKING 45–55 MIN. · LEVEL 1

17 beef vindaloo
with rice

- 1³/₄ pounds (800 g) beef chuck, cut into cubes
- 2 tablespoons vindaloo paste
- 1 cup (250 ml) beef stock
- 2 onions, thinly sliced
- 1¹/₂ cups (300 g) basmati rice

Combine the beef and vindaloo paste in a large frying pan over medium-high heat. Cook until aromatic, about 1 minute. Add 1 tablespoon of stock to deglaze the pan and transfer the beef to a medium saucepan.

Add the onions and remaining stock to the pan with the beef. Bring to a boil. Cover and simmer over low heat for 1 hour, stirring often. Uncover and simmer until the beef is very tender, about 30 more minutes.

Bring a large saucepan of salted water to a boil. Add the rice and cook over medium heat until tender, 10–15 minutes. Drain well. Serve hot with the beef vindaloo.

SERVES **4** • PREPARATION **10** MIN. • COOKING 1¹/₂ HR. • LEVEL **1**

18 veal escalopes
with parmesan cheese

- 1¼ pounds (600 g) small, thinly sliced veal escalopes (cut from the rump)
- 1 large egg
- Salt
- ⅓ cup (90 g) butter
- ¾ cup (90 g) Parmesan cheese, in small shavings
- ½ cup (120 ml) hot beef stock

Lightly pound the escalopes with a meat tenderizer so that they are thin and of even thickness.

Lightly beat the egg with a pinch of salt. Dip the escalopes in the egg mixture.

Heat the butter in a large frying pan over medium-high heat. Add the escalopes and sauté until pale golden brown on both sides, 2–3 minutes (depending on the thickness of the meat).

Arrange the escalopes in a single layer in a greased fireproof casserole. Cover with a layer of the Parmesan shavings. Add the hot stock, then cover and simmer over low heat until the cheese has melted, about 8–10 minutes. Serve hot.

SERVES 4 • PREPARATION 10 MIN. • COOKING 10–12 MIN. • LEVEL 1

Serve these escalopes hot with rice or mashed or roasted potatoes to soak up the cooking juices. Add a few leaves of fresh salad to lighten the dish.

19 orange-glazed chicken
with couscous

- Finely shredded zest and juice of 2 unwaxed oranges
- 2 tablespoons honey
- 4 boneless chicken breasts, with skin on
- 1½ cups (300 g) instant couscous
- 1½ cups (370 ml) hot chicken stock

Mix the orange juice and honey in a large bowl. Coat the chicken with this mixture. Cover and chill for 1 hour.

Put the couscous in a medium bowl. Add the chicken stock and orange zest. Cover the bowl and let stand for 10 minutes, until the couscous has absorbed the liquid. Fluff up with a fork.

Preheat a grill pan or barbecue on high. Grill the chicken until cooked through, about 5 minutes on each side. Slice the chicken and serve hot with the couscous.

SERVES 4 • PREPARATION 20 MIN. + 1 HR. TO MARINATE • COOKING 10 MIN. • LEVEL 1

20 balsamic chicken
with roasted tomatoes

- ½ cup (120 ml) balsamic vinegar
- 6 tablespoons (90 ml) extra-virgin olive oil
- 4 boneless chicken breasts, with skin on
- 16 cherry tomatoes
- Salt and freshly ground black pepper

Mix the vinegar and 4 tablespoons of oil in a bowl. Coat the chicken with this mixture. Cover and chill for 1 hour.

Preheat the oven to 350°F (180°C/gas 4). Put the tomatoes on a baking sheet and drizzle with the remaining oil. Season with salt and pepper. Roast for 10–15 minutes, until the tomatoes begin to soften.

Preheat a grill pan or barbecue on high. Grill the chicken until cooked through, about 5 minutes on each side. Slice and serve hot with the roasted tomatoes.

SERVES 4 • PREPARATION 20 MIN. + 1 HR. TO CHILL • COOKING 10–15 MIN. • LEVEL 1

1
chicken salad
with fruit

2
chicken salad with arugula
& white beans

3
chicken with
bell peppers

4
chicken burgers
with olive butter

5
crumbed chicken
with french fries

6
roasted lemon chicken
with potatoes

7
sweet & spicy chicken

8
citrus chicken
with arugula & feta

9
veal escalopes with
parmesan & fresh tomatoes

10
chicken tagine
with prunes

11
marengo chicken

12

veal stew
with milk & parsley

13

chicken casserole
with apricots

14

sausage casserole
with pineapple & potato

simple
recipes

15

pork loin with prunes

16

pork cutlets
with mustard crumb

17

pork chops
with prosciutto & cheese

18

pork loin
with milk & vinegar

19

highland stew

20

lamb & bell pepper stew

1 chicken salad
with fruit

- 4 cups (500 g) cooked chicken, cubed (leftover roast chicken or 2 grilled or poached chicken breasts)
- 4 stalks celery, sliced
- 1 cup (150 g) seedless red or green grapes, sliced
- 2 fresh peaches, peeled and cubed
- ½ cup (120 ml) mayonnaise
- ½ cup (120 ml) sour cream
- Salt and freshly ground black pepper
- Sprigs of parsley, to garnish

Combine the chicken, celery, grapes, and peaches in a large bowl and toss gently. Mix the mayonnaise and sour cream in a small bowl and pour over the salad. Season with salt and pepper.

Chill in the refrigerator for 30 minutes. Garnish with the parsley and serve.

SERVES 4 • PREPARATION 10 MIN. + 30 MIN. TO CHILL • LEVEL 1

2 chicken salad
with arugula & white beans

- $\frac{1}{3}$ cup (90 ml) freshly squeezed lemon juice
- 3 cloves garlic, finely chopped
- 2 tablespoons chopped fresh cilantro (coriander) + extra leaves, to garnish
- 1 tablespoon brown sugar
- $\frac{1}{2}$ cup (120 ml) extra-virgin olive oil
- Salt and freshly ground black pepper
- 2 boneless skinless chicken breasts, sliced
- 1 (14-ounce/400-g) can white kidney or cannellini beans, drained
- 2 cups (100 g) baby arugula (rocket) leaves

Preheat a grill pan or barbecue on high. Whisk the lemon juice, garlic, chopped cilantro, sugar, and oil in a small bowl. Season with salt and pepper.

Grill the chicken until cooked through, 5–7 minutes on each side. During cooking, turn the chicken and baste with half the lemon and oil mixture.

Toss the beans, arugula, and remaining lemon and oil mixture in a bowl. Add the chicken and toss gently. Serve warm.

SERVES 4 • PREPARATION 15 MIN. • COOKING 10–12 MIN. • LEVEL 1

3 chicken
with bell peppers

- ¼ cup (60 ml) extra-virgin olive oil
- 2 cloves garlic, finely chopped
- 1 chicken, about 3 pounds (1.5 kg), cut into 8 pieces
- Salt and freshly ground black pepper
- ½ cup (120 ml) dry white wine
- 14 ounces (400 g) firm, ripe tomatoes, peeled and chopped
- 3 medium green bell peppers (capsicums), chopped into squares
- Fresh cilantro (coriander) leaves, to sprinkle
- Garlic mash, to serve (see page 285)

Heat the oil in a large frying pan over medium heat. Add the garlic and sauté until pale golden brown, 3–4 minutes. Add the chicken pieces and sauté over medium-high heat until golden brown all over, about 5 minutes. Season with salt and pepper.

Pour in the wine and simmer until it has evaporated. Add the tomatoes and bell peppers and simmer until the chicken and bell peppers are tender and the tomatoes have reduced, about 35 minutes.

Sprinkle with the cilantro and serve hot with the garlic mash.

SERVES 4 · PREPARATION 15 MIN. · COOKING 50 MIN. · LEVEL 1

If liked, use yellow or red bell peppers instead of the green, or use a mixture of colors. If you like spicy dishes, add a finely chopped chile together with the bell peppers.

4 chicken burgers
with olive butter

- 3/4 cup (100 g) black olive paste (tapenade)
- 1/2 cup (120 g) butter, at room temperature
- 1 clove garlic, finely chopped
- 2 pounds (1 kg) ground (minced) chicken
- 1 shallot, finely chopped
- 3 tablespoons finely chopped fresh thyme
- Salt and freshly ground black pepper
- 1/4 cup (60 ml) extra-virgin olive oil
- 2 cups (100 g) arugula (rocket), to serve
- Whole black olives, to serve

Mix the olive paste, butter, and garlic in a small bowl. Place the mixture on a sheet of aluminum foil and shape into a log. Wrap in the foil and put in the freezer.

Place the chicken in a bowl with the shallot and thyme. Season with salt and pepper. Divide the mixture into 4–6 portions and shape into burgers.

Fry the burgers in the oil in a large frying pan over medium-high heat until cooked, 3–4 minutes on each side. Put the burgers on a bed of arugula and garnish with the olives. Slice the frozen butter and place on top of the burgers. Serve hot.

SERVES 4–6 • PREPARATION 15 MIN. • COOKING 6–8 MIN. • LEVEL 1

5 crumbed chicken
with french fries

- 2 cups (120 g) fresh bread crumbs
- 2 tablespoons finely chopped fresh parsley
- 2 tablespoons finely chopped fresh chives
- Salt and freshly ground black pepper
- 4 boneless skinless chicken breast halves
- 1/2 cup (75 g) all-purpose (plain) flour
- 2 large eggs, lightly beaten
- 2 tablespoons extra-virgin olive oil
- Lemon wedges, to serve
- French fries (potato chips), to serve (optional)

Mix the bread crumbs, parsley, and chives in a small bowl. Season with salt and pepper.

Flatten the chicken slightly with a meat tenderizer. Dip the chicken in the flour, then in the eggs, followed by the bread crumbs.

Fry the chicken in batches in the oil in a large frying pan over medium heat until golden and crisp, 3–5 minutes on each side. Serve hot with the lemon wedges and French fries, if liked.

SERVES 4 • PREPARATION 10 MIN. • COOKING 6–10 MIN • LEVEL 1

6 roasted lemon chicken
with potatoes

- 1 tablespoon finely chopped fresh sage
- 1 tablespoon finely chopped fresh rosemary
- 2 cloves garlic, finely chopped
- 1 teaspoon salt
- 1 teaspoon freshly ground black pepper
- 1 chicken, weighing about 4 pounds (2 kg)
- 1 whole unwaxed lemon
- $\frac{1}{4}$ cup (60 ml) extra-virgin olive oil
- 1$\frac{1}{2}$ pounds (750 g) roasting potatoes

Preheat the oven to 400°F (200°C/gas 6). Combine the sage, rosemary, garlic, salt, and pepper in a bowl. Mix well, then use to season the chicken inside and out.

Prick the lemon thoroughly with a fork and insert into the abdominal cavity of the chicken. Place the chicken in a roasting pan and drizzle with the oil. Bake for 15 minutes, then add the potatoes.

Turn the chicken and potatoes every 15 minutes, basting with the oil and cooking juices. When cooked, the chicken should be very tender, the meat should come off the bone easily, and the skin should be crisp, about 1 hour.

Transfer to a heated serving dish and serve hot.

SERVES 4–6 · PREPARATION 15 MIN. · COOKING 1 HR. · LEVEL 1

This is an Italian recipe for roasting chicken. Inserting a lemon inside the cavity of the chicken both absorbs fat and adds flavor.

7 sweet & spicy chicken

- ½ cup (120 ml) honey
- ¼ cup (60 ml) chile paste
- Salt and freshly ground black pepper
- 4 boneless skinless chicken breast halves
- 3 cups (150 g) baby spinach leaves
- 16 cherry tomatoes, halved

Mix the honey, chile paste, salt, and pepper in a cup. Smear over the chicken. Place in a bowl, cover, and chill for 1 hour. Toss the spinach and tomatoes in a bowl.

Preheat a grill pan or barbecue on high. Grill the chicken until cooked through, about 5 minutes on each side. Serve hot with the spinach and tomatoes.

SERVES **4** • PREPARATION **10** MIN. **+ 1** HR. TO MARINATE • COOKING **10** MIN. • LEVEL **1**

8 citrus chicken
with arugula & feta

- 3 tablespoons extra-virgin olive oil
- 6 boneless chicken thighs, with skin, halved
- 2 red onions, thinly sliced
- Freshly squeezed juice of 1 orange
- Freshly squeezed juice of 1 lemon
- ½ cup (50 g) black olives
- 3 ounces (90 g) feta cheese, crumbled
- 1 bunch arugula (rocket), trimmed

Heat the oil in a large frying pan over medium-high heat. Sauté the chicken, turning once, until golden, about 10 minutes.

Add the onions and sauté until just tender, about 3 minutes. Add the orange and lemon juices. Cover and bring to a boil. Sprinkle with the olives and feta. Cover and cook for 1 minute.

Arrange the chicken on serving plates, drizzle with the pan juices, and serve hot with the arugula.

SERVES 4 • PREPARATION 10 MIN. • COOKING 15 MIN. • LEVEL 1

9 veal escalopes
with parmesan & fresh tomatoes

- 1¼ pounds (600 g) small, thinly sliced veal escalopes (cut from the rump)
- ½ cup (75 g) all-purpose (plain) flour
- ¼ cup (60 ml) extra-virgin olive oil
- 2 tablespoons butter
- Salt and freshly ground black pepper
- ½ cup (120 ml) dry white wine
- 2 shallots, coarsely chopped
- 3–4 medium tomatoes, peeled and diced
- 4 ounces (120 g) Parmesan cheese, flaked
- 2 tablespoons finely chopped fresh parsley
- 2 tablespoons finely chopped fresh basil

Lightly pound the escalopes with a meat tenderizer so that they are thin and of even thickness. Dredge in the flour, shaking off any excess.

Heat the oil and butter in a large frying pan over medium heat. Add the escalopes and brown on both sides, about 5 minutes (depending on the thickness of the meat). Season with salt and pepper. Pour in the wine and simmer until it evaporates. Remove the escalopes and set aside in a warm oven.

Add the shallots to the pan and lightly brown. Add the tomatoes, season with salt and pepper, and simmer until the tomatoes reduce, about 10 minutes.

Return the escalopes to the pan and sprinkle with the Parmesan, parsley, and basil. Turn off the heat, cover, and let stand for a few minutes. Serve hot.

SERVES 4 • PREPARATION 15 MIN. • COOKING 25–30 MIN. • LEVEL 1

Serve these escalopes with some boiled potatoes or rice and a green salad for a complete and simple meal.

10 chicken tagine
with prunes

- 1 chicken, weighing about 4 pounds (2 kg), cut into 6–8 pieces
- 3 large onions, sliced
- $^{1}/_{3}$ cup (90 g) butter
- 1 stick cinnamon
- $^{1}/_{4}$ teaspoon saffron threads
- Salt and freshly ground black pepper
- $1^{1}/_{2}$ cups (375 ml) water
- 1 cup (200 g) pitted prunes
- 2 tablespoons honey
- 2 tablespoons freshly squeezed lemon juice
- 1 tablespoon sesame seeds
- $^{3}/_{4}$ cup (120 g) almonds
- Freshly prepared couscous, to serve

Place the chicken, onions, butter, cinnamon, saffron, salt, pepper, and water in a large saucepan. Cover and simmer over low heat for 40–45 minutes, stirring occasionally. Remove the chicken and keep warm.

Add the prunes to the liquid and simmer until the prunes have softened, 10–15 minutes. Add the honey and lemon juice and simmer over low heat until reduced by half, about 10 minutes. Return the chicken to the pan and simmer for 10 minutes. Sprinkle with the sesame seeds and almonds. Serve hot with the couscous.

SERVES **4–6** • PREPARATION **15** MIN. • COOKING **70–80** MIN. • LEVEL **1**

11 marengo chicken

- 1 chicken, weighing about 4 pounds (2 kg) cut into 6–8 pieces
- ¼ cup (60 g) butter
- Salt and freshly ground black pepper
- Dash of nutmeg + extra, to dust
- ½ cup (120 ml) dry white wine
- 1 tablespoon all-purpose (plain) flour
- 1 cup (250 ml) beef stock
- Freshly squeezed juice of ½ lemon

Place the chicken in a heavy-bottomed pan with the butter and sauté over medium-high heat until lightly browned, about 5 minutes. Season with salt, pepper, and nutmeg.

Discard any liquid in the pan. Add the wine and stir in the flour. Simmer over low heat until the chicken is tender, about 50 minutes. Add the stock as required during cooking to keep the chicken moist.

Arrange the chicken on a serving dish and drizzle with the lemon juice. Serve hot, dusted with extra nutmeg.

SERVES 4–6 • PREPARATION 15 MIN. • COOKING 1 HR. • LEVEL 1

12 veal stew
with milk & parsley

- 2 pounds (1 kg) lean suckling veal, cut in bite-size pieces
- $1/4$ cup (60 ml) extra-virgin olive oil
- 2 cloves garlic, finely chopped
- 2 tablespoons finely chopped fresh parsley + extra, to garnish
- Salt and freshly ground black pepper
- 1 cup (250 ml) milk
- 1 cup (250 ml) beef stock

Remove any pieces of fat from the veal. Heat the oil in a large heavy-bottomed pan over medium heat. Add the garlic and parsley and sauté for 2–3 minutes.

Add the meat and sauté until lightly browned, about 5 minutes. Season with salt and pepper. Pour in the milk and beef stock. The meat should be almost, but not completely, covered. Reduce the heat and partially cover the pan, leaving space for the liquid to reduce a little. Cook very slowly, stirring frequently, until the veal is tender and a tasty, dense sauce has formed, about 1 hour.

Transfer to a heated serving dish and serve hot, garnished with a little extra parsley.

SERVES **6** • PREPARATION **15** MIN. • COOKING **60–70** MIN. • LEVEL **1**

This stew is delicious served with steamed or boiled potatoes or rice, or with slabs of freshly baked bread. You need something to mop up the tasty sauce.

13 chicken casserole
with apricots

- 2 pounds (1 kg) chicken pieces
- 1 (14-ounce/400-g) can apricots, drained, juice reserved
- 1 pound (500 g) tiny new potatoes, scrubbed
- 1½ cups (250 g) frozen peas
- Handful of coarsely chopped fresh cilantro (coriander)
- 1 (4-ounce/120-g) package powdered onion soup
- Freshly ground black pepper
- About 1 cup (250 ml) dry white wine
- Freshly cooked rice, to serve

Preheat the oven to 375°F (190°C/gas 5). Place the chicken in a casserole dish. Cover with the apricots, potatoes, peas, and cilantro. Sprinkle with the powdered soup and season lightly with pepper.

Add enough wine to the reserved apricot juice to make 1½ cups (370 ml) of liquid. Pour over the ingredients in the casserole dish and let stand for 15 minutes.

Stir gently, then cover tightly. Bake for 1 hour, until the chicken is very tender. Check from time to time, adding more wine if the sauce is dry. Serve hot with the rice.

SERVES 4–6 · PREPARATION 15 MIN. + 15 MIN. TO STAND · COOKING 1 HR. · LEVEL 1

14 sausage casserole
with pineapple & potato

- 6–8 sausages, cut into bite-size chunks
- 1$\frac{1}{2}$ pounds (750 g) potatoes, peeled and cut into small cubes
- 1 (15-ounce/450-g) can pineapple chunks, drained, juice reserved
- 1 large onion, coarsely chopped
- 2 large carrots, sliced
- 2 large tomatoes, sliced
- Water
- 2 tablespoons brown sugar
- 2 tablespoons cornstarch (cornflour)
- Salt and freshly ground black pepper
- 1 tablespoon butter

Preheat the oven to 350°F (180°C/gas 4). Layer the sausages, potatoes, pineapple chunks, onion, carrots, and tomatoes in a casserole dish.

Add enough water to the pineapple juice to make 1$\frac{1}{4}$ cups (300 ml). Put $\frac{1}{2}$ cup (120 ml) of the pineapple liquid in a small bowl. Add the brown sugar and cornstarch and stir until smooth. Season with salt and pepper. Add the remaining pineapple liquid and stir until smooth. Pour the cornstarch mixture over the ingredients in the casserole. Top with the butter.

Cover and bake until tender, about 1 hour. Serve hot.

SERVES 6 • PREPARATION 15 MIN. • COOKING 1 HR. • LEVEL 1

15 pork loin
with prunes

- 20–25 dried prunes, pitted
- $^1/_2$ cup (120 ml) cognac
- 2 pounds (1 kg) boneless pork loin
- Salt and freshly ground black pepper
- 8 long sprigs fresh rosemary
- 2 tablespoons butter
- $^1/_4$ cup (60 ml) extra-virgin olive oil
- $^3/_4$ cup (180 ml) dry white wine
- 1 cup (250 ml) beef stock

Cut 10 prunes in halves or quarters. Place in a bowl with the cognac, diluted with enough water to cover the fruit. Set aside to marinate for 30 minutes. Drain well.

Preheat the oven to 350°F (180°C/gas 4). Use a sharp knife to make incisions in the pork. Fill with a little salt and pepper and the chopped prunes.

Place the rosemary on the meat and tie with kitchen string. Season with salt and pepper.

Heat the butter and oil in an ovenproof pan over medium heat. As soon as the butter foams, add the pork and brown all over, 5–8 minutes. Transfer to the hot oven and bake until tender and cooked through, 1–2 hours. Halfway through cooking, pour the wine over the meat and add the remaining prunes. Continue cooking, adding some stock if the pan dries out.

Serve hot or at room temperature with the sauce (heated, if the meat is lukewarm).

SERVES 4 • PREPARATION 15 MIN. + 30 MIN. TO MARINATE COOKING 1–2 HR. • LEVEL 1

Pork goes beautifully with many types of fruit. It is especially good with sweet dried prunes.

16 pork cutlets
with mustard crumb

- ¼ cup (30 g) all-purpose (plain) flour
- 2 teaspoons dry mustard powder
- 4 pork cutlets, cut in half lengthwise
- 1 large egg, lightly beaten
- 1 cup (150 g) fine dry bread crumbs
- ¼ cup (60 ml) extra-virgin olive oil
- Green salad, to serve

Mix the flour and mustard powder in a small bowl. Coat the pork in the flour mixture, shaking off any excess. Dip into the beaten egg and coat in the bread crumbs.

Heat the oil in a large deep frying pan until very hot. Fry the pork in batches until golden, about 3 minutes each side. Serve the pork with the salad.

SERVES **4** · PREPARATION **10** MIN. · COOKING **10–15** MIN. · LEVEL **1**

17 pork chops
with prosciutto & cheese

- 4 pork loin chops, bone-in
- 1 cup (150 g) all-purpose (plain) flour, seasoned with salt and freshly ground black pepper
- 1 large egg, lightly beaten
- 1 cup (150 g) fine dry bread crumbs
- 3 tablespoons butter
- 1 tablespoon extra-virgin olive oil
- 4 slices prosciutto
- 2 ounces (60 g) Parmesan cheese, thinly sliced
- 4 tablespoons (60 ml) light (single) cream

Dip the chops in the seasoned flour until well coated, shaking off any excess. Dip in the egg and then in the bread crumbs.

Heat the butter and oil in a large frying pan over medium heat. Add the chops and fry until cooked through and a thick golden crust forms, about 5 minutes on each side. Drain well on paper towels.

Preheat an overhead broiler (grill). Place the chops on a baking sheet. Top each one with a slice of prosciutto, some Parmesan, and 1 tablespoon of cream. Broil until the cheese has melted, about 2 minutes. Serve hot.

SERVES 4 • PREPARATION 10 MIN. • COOKING 15 MIN. • LEVEL 1

18 pork loin
with milk & vinegar

- 2¼ pounds (1.2 kg) boneless pork loin roast
- Salt and freshly ground black pepper
- 2 tablespoons butter
- ¼ cup (60 ml) extra-virgin olive oil
- 1 sprig rosemary
- 1 onion, finely chopped
- ¾ cup (180 ml) dry white vinegar
- 1¾ cups (430 ml) milk
- 1 beef stock cube, crumbled
- Boiled potatoes, to serve

Season the pork with salt and pepper. Roll and tie with a few twists of kitchen string.

Heat the butter and oil in a heavy-bottomed pan with the rosemary. When the butter foams, add the onion and sauté until softened, 3–4 minutes. Add the pork and lightly brown all over, about 10 minutes.

Pour the vinegar over the pork and simmer until it has evaporated. Add the milk and beef stock cube. Partially cover the pan and simmer for 1 hour, turning the meat from time to time. When cooked, the sauce in the pan should be well-reduced and thick.

Slice the pork, transfer to a heated serving dish, and spoon the sauce over the top. Serve hot with the potatoes and the pan juices spooned over the top.

SERVES 4–6 · PREPARATION 10 MIN. · COOKING 75 MIN. · LEVEL 1

Pork loin roast is cut from the back, or loin, of a pig. If it is cut from the center it will still have the ribs attached. A boneless pork loin roast has no ribs attached and is usually rolled and tied with kitchen string to stop it from falling apart.

19 highland stew

- 1½ pounds (750 g) stew beef, cut into small chunks
- 2 tablespoons all-purpose (plain) flour
- Salt and freshly ground black pepper
- ¼ cup (60 ml) extra-virgin olive oil
- 1 large onion, coarsely chopped
- 4 medium potatoes, peeled and cubed
- 2 large carrots, coarsely chopped
- ¼ rutabaga turnip, peeled and coarsely chopped (about 2 cups)
- 1½ cups (370 ml) beef stock

Sprinkle the beef with the flour. Season with salt and pepper. Heat the oil in a large heavy-bottomed pan over medium heat. Add the beef in small batches and sauté until browned all over, 8–10 minutes.

Add the onion, potatoes, carrots, and rutabaga and sauté over medium heat until lightly browned, 8–10 minutes. Pour in the stock. Season with salt and pepper. Simmer over low heat until the meat is very tender, 1–2 hours. Serve hot.

SERVES **4** • PREPARATION **20** MIN. • COOKING **1–2** HR. • LEVEL **1**

20 lamb & bell pepper stew

- 4 tablespoons (60 ml) extra-virgin olive oil
- 2 pounds (1 kg) lamb shoulder, boned and cut into small cubes
- Salt and freshly ground black pepper
- 1 cup (150 g) diced pancetta
- 2 cloves garlic, finely chopped
- 1 large onion, chopped
- 3 red and yellow bell peppers (capsicums), chopped
- $\frac{1}{2}$ cup (120 ml) white wine
- 1 (14-ounce/400-g) can tomatoes, with juice
- 2 tablespoons finely chopped fresh parsley

Heat 2 tablespoons of oil in a large saucepan over medium heat. Add the lamb and sauté until browned, 8–10 minutes. Season with salt and pepper. Set aside.

Heat the remaining 2 tablespoons of oil over medium heat in the same pan. Add the pancetta, garlic, and onion and sauté until softened, 3–4 minutes. Add the bell peppers and simmer for 5 minutes. Pour in the wine. When it has evaporated, add the tomatoes, partially cover the pan, and simmer for 15 minutes. Add the lamb and parsley, season, and simmer until tender, about 40 minutes. Serve hot.

SERVES 4 • PREPARATION 20 MIN. • COOKING 70–75 MIN. • LEVEL 1

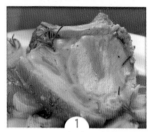

1

roasted pork
with vegetables & gravy

2

roasted lamb
with vegetables

3

pollo alla cacciatora
(hunter's chicken stew)

TOP
20

4

chicken provençal

5

coq au vin
(french chicken & red wine stew)

6

cajun jambalaya
(louisiana meat & fish stew)

7

carpaccio
(italian raw veal salad)

8

souvlaki
(greek skewers)

9

lamb tagine
with prunes

10

milanese fried veal chops

11

veal saltimbocca
(roman veal escalopes)

vitello tonnato
(veal with tuna sauce)

blanquette de veau
(french veal stew)

beef bourguignon
(burgundy beef stew)

classic
recipes

ossobuchi alla milanese
(milan-style braised beef shanks)

pot au feu
(french boiled meats)

bollito misto
(italian boiled meats)

chili con carne

beef rendang
(indonesian beef curry)

lamb rogan josh
(indian lamb curry)

1 roasted pork
with vegetables & gravy

- 1 bone-in pork loin roast, about 5 pounds (2.5 kg)
- 4 cloves garlic, thinly sliced
- 1 teaspoon salt
- $\frac{1}{2}$ teaspoon black pepper
- 2 tablespoons fresh or dried rosemary leaves
- 4 sweet potatoes, peeled and cut into chunks
- 1 small rutabaga (swede), peeled and chopped
- 4 parsnips, peeled and sliced
- 4 carrots, sliced
- $\frac{1}{4}$ cup (60 ml) extra-virgin olive oil
- 1 tablespoon cornstarch (cornflour)
- 3 tablespoons cold water
- $1\frac{1}{2}$ cups (375 ml) boiling water

Preheat the oven to 350°F (180°C/gas 4). Cut slits in the pork and insert slices of garlic. Mix the salt, pepper, and rosemary in a cup and rub over the pork. Place the pork, fat-side up, in a roasting pan. Add the vegetables and drizzle with the oil. Season with salt and pepper.

Roast for $1\frac{1}{2}$ hours, until the meat is tender and the vegetables are cooked and crisp. Drain and discard the fat from the roasting pan. Place the pan over medium heat. Mix the cornstarch in a small bowl with the cold water. Add to the roasting pan with the boiling water. Stir, scraping the bottom of the pan, and simmer until thickened. Serve hot.

SERVES 6–8 • PREPARATION 20 MIN. • $1\frac{1}{2}$ HR. • LEVEL 1

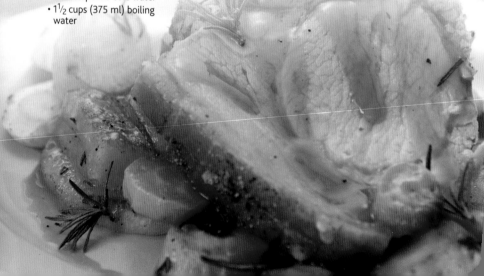

2 roasted lamb
with vegetables

- 4 large onions, coarsely chopped
- 4 tablespoons (60 ml) extra-virgin olive oil
- 3 pounds (1.5 kg) leg or shoulder of lamb, cut into 6–8 pieces
- 12 cherry tomatoes
- 1¼ pounds (600 g) potatoes, peeled and cut into ¼-inch (5-mm) slices
- Salt and freshly ground black pepper
- Sprigs of fresh rosemary

Preheat the oven to 350°F (180°C/gas 4). Sauté the onions in 1 tablespoon of oil in a large frying pan over medium heat until softened, 3–4 minutes. Add the lamb and brown all over, 5–10 minutes.

Transfer to a roasting pan. Add the tomatoes and potatoes. Season with salt and pepper and sprinkle with the rosemary. Drizzle with the remaining 3 tablespoons of oil. Roast until the lamb and potatoes are cooked, about 50 minutes. Serve hot.

SERVES 4 • PREPARATION 15 MIN. • COOKING 55–65 MIN. • LEVEL 1

3 pollo alla cacciatora
(hunter's chicken stew)

- 1 chicken, about 4–5 pounds (2–2.5 kg) cut in 6–8 pieces
- 6 tablespoons (90 ml) extra-virgin olive oil
- Freshly squeezed juice of 1 lemon
- Salt and freshly ground black pepper
- 1 onion, coarsely chopped
- 1 carrot, coarsely chopped
- 1 stalk celery, coarsely chopped
- $^{1}/_{2}$ cup (120 ml) dry white wine
- 2 pounds (1 kg) tomatoes, peeled and chopped
- $^{1}/_{2}$ cup (120 ml) cold water
- $1^{1}/_{2}$ cups (150 g) black olives
- Coarsely chopped fresh parsley, to garnish

Place the chicken in a large bowl and drizzle with 3 tablespoons of oil and the lemon juice. Season with salt and a generous grinding of pepper. Marinate in the refrigerator for at least 4 hours, or overnight.

Heat the remaining 3 tablespoons of oil in a large, deep frying pan over medium heat. Add the onion, carrot, and celery and sauté until softened a little, about 5 minutes. Add the chicken pieces and sauté until golden, 5–8 minutes.

Pour in the wine and simmer until it evaporates, stirring frequently. Add the tomatoes and water. Cover the pan, decrease the heat to low, and continue to cook, stirring frequently. After 15 minutes add the olives. Simmer gently over low heat until the chicken is tender, about 20–30 more minutes. Serve hot, garnished with parsley.

SERVES 4–6 • PREPARATION 20 MIN. + 4–12 HR. TO MARINATE
COOKING 1 HR. • LEVEL 1

Pollo alla cacciatora is a very popular, traditional Italian dish. There are about as many versions of the recipe as there are cooks, so feel free to add your own variations. Serve hot with boiled or steamed potatoes or rice or with freshly made polenta.

4 chicken provençal

- ¼ cup (60 ml) extra-virgin olive oil
- 1 chicken, about 4 pounds (2 kg), cut into 6–8 pieces
- Salt and freshly ground black pepper
- 1 onion, finely chopped
- 3 cloves garlic, finely chopped
- 6 firm-ripe tomatoes, peeled and coarsely chopped
- 2 cups (500 ml) dry white wine
- 1 tablespoon finely chopped fresh rosemary
- 1 tablespoon finely chopped fresh thyme + extra, to garnish
- 1 cup (100 g) black olives

Heat the oil in a large saucepan over high heat. Add the chicken and sauté until golden, 8–10 minutes. Season with salt and pepper. Set the chicken aside.

In the same pan, simmer the onion, garlic, and tomatoes until the tomatoes begin to break down, about 10 minutes. Season with salt. Lower the heat and pour in the wine. Stir in the rosemary, thyme, and olives. Simmer for 10 minutes. Return the chicken to the pan and season with salt and pepper. Cover and simmer over low heat until the chicken is very tender, 30–40 minutes. Serve hot garnished with thyme.

SERVES 6 • PREPARATION 20 MIN. • COOKING 60–70 MIN. • LEVEL 1

5 coq au vin
(french chicken & red wine stew)

- 3 tablespoons extra-virgin olive oil
- 1 chicken, about 4–5 pounds (2–2.5 kg), cut into 8 pieces
- 2 tablespoons all-purpose (plain) flour
- 2 cups (240 g) diced bacon
- 8 ounces (250 g) button mushrooms
- 2 onions, finely chopped
- 2 shallots, finely chopped
- 3 cloves garlic, finely chopped
- 1 teaspoon tomato paste (concentrate)
- 1 bouquet garni + fresh herbs, to garnish
- Salt and freshly ground black pepper
- 2 cups (500 ml) dry red wine
- 1½ cups (375 ml) beef stock

Heat the oil in a large saucepan over medium heat. Add the chicken and sauté until golden, 8–10 minutes. Sprinkle with the flour, letting it soak up the oil. Remove and set aside.

Add the bacon, mushrooms, onions, and shallots to the same pan and sauté over medium heat until lightly browned, about 10 minutes. Add the garlic, tomato paste, and bouquet garni. Season with salt and pepper. Pour in the wine and stock. Return the chicken to the pan. Cover and simmer over low heat until very tender, 30–45 minutes. Garnish with the herbs and serve hot.

SERVES 4–6 • PREPARATION 20 MIN. • COOKING 55–70 MIN. • LEVEL 1

6 cajun jambalaya
(louisiana meat & fish stew)

- ¹/₄ cup (60 ml) extra-virgin olive oil
- 1 onion, chopped
- 3 mixed colored bell peppers (capsicums), chopped
- 5 cloves garlic, finely chopped
- 4 chorizo sausages, thickly sliced
- 2 pounds (1 kg) chicken pieces
- 2 hot chiles, 1 red, 1 yellow, chopped
- 1 pound (500 g) American-style rice
- 1 teaspoon chile powder
- 2 tablespoons turmeric
- 2 tablespoons Cajun spices
- 4 cups (1 liter) chicken stock
- 4 cups (500 g) chopped mixed vegetables, such as carrots, peas, green beans, brussels sprouts, zucchini (courgettes)
- 1 pound (500 g) large shrimp (king prawns) or crayfish
- Salt and freshly ground black pepper

Heat the oil in a large saucepan over medium heat. Add the onion, bell peppers, garlic, chorizo, and chicken pieces and sauté for about 10 minutes.

Add the chiles and rice and stir well. Add the chile powder, turmeric, and Cajun spices and mix in so the rice is well coated with the flavors. Pour in the chicken stock and bring to a simmer.

Add the mixed vegetables and bring to a boil, then turn the heat down to a simmer. When the rice has been cooking for about 10 minutes, add the shrimp or crayfish. Simmer for 45–60 minutes more, until the chicken is very tender. Serve hot.

SERVES 6–8 • PREPARATION 20 MIN. • COOKING 65–80 MIN. LEVEL 2

Jambalaya is a classic dish from Louisiana. It combines the French and Spanish influences of the original European settlers of that state. Our recipe is a Cajun variation and does not contain tomatoes. To make a creole jambalaya, add tomatoes and use a smoked andouille sausage instead of the chorizo.

7 carpaccio
(italian raw veal salad)

- 1 pound (500 g) very fresh beef fillet
- 2 cups (100 g) arugula (rocket)
- 1 tablespoon balsamic vinegar
- 3 tablespoons extra-virgin olive oil
- 2 ounces (60 g) Parmesan or pecorino cheese, shaved
- Salt and freshly ground black pepper

Wrap the beef tightly in plastic wrap (cling film) and freeze until firm, about 2 hours. Use a very sharp knife to cut the beef very thinly into ⅛-inch (3-mm) slices.

Put the arugula in a bowl and toss with the balsamic vinegar and oil. Lay the beef slices slightly overlapping on each serving dish and top with the arugula and shavings of cheese. Season with salt and pepper. Serve at room temperature.

SERVES 6 · PREPARATION 10 MIN. + 2 HR. TO FREEZE · LEVEL 1

8 souvlaki
(greek skewers)

Tzatziki
- 1 cup (250 ml) plain yogurt
- 1 clove garlic, minced
- 1 tablespoon lemon juice
- 1 cucumber, peeled, seeded, and finely chopped
- 1 tablespoon finely chopped fresh mint
- Salt

Lamb
- ⅓ cup (90 ml) extra-virgin olive oil
- 2 tablespoons lemon juice
- 2 tablespoons red wine vinegar
- 2 tablespoons dried oregano
- 1 clove garlic, minced
- 1 teaspoon ground cumin
- Salt and freshly ground black pepper
- 1½ pounds (750 g) lamb leg, boned, cut into cubes
- Mixed salad and pita bread, to serve

Tzatziki Combine the yogurt, garlic, and lemon juice in a small bowl. Add the cucumber and mint and season with salt. Cover with plastic wrap (cling film) and chill.

Lamb Combine the oil, lemon juice, vinegar, oregano, garlic, and cumin in a large bowl. Season with salt and pepper. Add the lamb and toss to coat. Cover with plastic wrap and refrigerate overnight.

Preheat a grill pan or barbecue on high. Drain the lamb, reserving the marinade. Thread the lamb onto metal skewers. Cook, basting frequently with the marinade, until cooked, about 4–5 minutes each side. Serve hot with pita bread, salad, and tzatziki.

SERVES 4–6 • PREPARATION 15 MIN. + 12 HR. TO MARINATE
COOKING 8–10 MIN. • LEVEL 1

9 lamb tagine
with prunes

- 4 tablespoons (60 ml) extra-virgin olive oil
- 2 large onions, chopped
- 2 pounds (1 kg) lean leg of lamb, diced
- 2 cups (500 ml) cold water + extra, as needed
- Salt and freshly ground black pepper
- $1/2$ teaspoon ground coriander
- $1/2$ teaspoon ground cinnamon
- 1 cinnamon stick
- $1/2$ teaspoon ground cumin
- 1 teaspoon ginger
- Pinch saffron threads, soaked in 1 tablespoon water
- 16 prunes, soaked in warm water
- 4 tablespoons clear honey
- 1 tablespoon orange flower water
- 2 tablespoons cilantro (coriander) leaves, to garnish
- Freshly made couscous, to serve

Heat 2 tablespoons of oil in a large saucepan over medium heat. Add the onion and lamb and sauté until the meat is well browned, about 10 minutes. Pour in the water. The meat should just be covered; add more water as required.

Season with salt and pepper, add the 2 remaining tablespoons of oil, coriander, cinnamon, cinnamon stick, cumin, ginger, and saffron threads and water to the pan and bring to a boil. Decrease the heat to low, cover, and simmer for about 2 hours.

Add the soaked prunes and leave to simmer for 20 more minutes.

Stir in the honey and sprinkle the tagine with orange flower water and cilantro. Serve hot with the couscous.

SERVES **4–6** • PREPARATION **20** MIN. • COOKING **2**$1/2$ HR. • LEVEL **1**

Tagines are a type of fragrant stew from North Africa. They take their name from the traditional earthenware pot in which they are cooked.

10 milanese fried veal chops

- 4 large veal chops, bone-in
- 2 large eggs, lightly beaten
- 1½ cups (200 g) fine dry bread crumbs
- ½ cup (120 g) butter
- 1 tablespoon extra-virgin olive oil
- Salt
- Lemon wedges, to garnish

Lightly pound the veal with a meat tenderizer so that it is of even thickness. Dip in the eggs and then in the bread crumbs. Press down well so that the bread crumbs stick all over.

Heat the butter and oil in a large frying pan over medium-high heat. Add the chops and fry until a thick golden crust forms, 2–3 minutes. Turn and cook in the same way on the other side. If the chops don't all fit in the pan in a single layer, cook them in two pans or in two batches.

Drain well on paper towels and season with salt. Garnish with the lemon wedges and serve hot.

SERVES 4 • PREPARATION 10 MIN. • COOKING 10 MIN. • LEVEL 1

11 veal saltimbocca
(roman veal escalopes)

- 8 veal escalopes, about 1¼ pounds (600 g)
- ¼ cup (60 g) butter, cut up
- 8 slices prosciutto
- 8 whole sage leaves + 1 tablespoon coarsely chopped fresh sage + extra whole leaves, to garnish
- Salt
- ½ cup (120 ml) dry white wine

Lightly pound the veal with a meat tenderizer so that it is thin and of even thickness. Melt the butter in a large frying pan over high heat. Cook the veal until browned, 2–3 minutes on each side.

Remove from the pan, top each escalope with a slice of prosciutto and two sage leaves. Secure with toothpicks. Return the veal to the pan with the butter and add the chopped sage. Cook over medium heat for 1 minute. Season with salt. Turn up the heat. Pour in the wine and let it evaporate. Discard the toothpicks and serve hot, garnished with the whole sage leaves.

SERVES 4 • PREPARATION 10 MIN. • COOKING 10 MIN. • LEVEL 2

12 vitello tonnato
(veal with tuna sauce)

- 2 pounds (1 kg) lean veal roast, preferably cut from the rump
- 1 carrot
- 1 stalk celery
- 1 bay leaf
- 1 onion
- 2 cloves
- Salt and freshly ground black pepper
- 5 ounces (150 g) canned tuna, drained
- 1 cup (250 ml) mayonnaise
- 2 tablespoons capers + extra, to garnish
- Freshly squeezed juice of 1 lemon + wedges of lemon, to garnish
- $\frac{1}{4}$ cup (60 ml) extra-virgin olive oil

Remove any fat from the meat and tie firmly with kitchen string. Put the meat, carrot, celery, bay leaf, and onion stuck with the cloves in a pot with just enough boiling water to cover the meat. Season with salt, cover, and simmer for 2 hours. Leave the veal to cool in the cooking water, 1–2 hours.

Put the tuna in a food processor with the mayonnaise, capers, lemon juice, oil, salt, and pepper. Blend until smooth.

Remove the veal from the cooking water, draining well. Slice thinly, transfer to a serving dish, and spoon the sauce over the top. Garnish with capers and wedges of lemon. Chill in the refrigerator for 6 hours.

Serve by itself as an appetizer or with boiled vegetables as a light lunch or main course.

SERVES 6–8 • PREPARATION 30 MIN. + 7–8 HR. TO COOL & CHILL
COOKING 2 HR. • LEVEL 2

This wonderful dish requires careful preparation, but the end result is well worth the effort. Firstly, the veal needs to cool in its cooking water (to stop it from becoming tough). Furthermore, the sauce should be spooned over the cool meat and left for several hours before serving. Prepare it a day ahead, so that the veal and tuna sauce are fully blended.

13 blanquette de veau
(french veal stew)

- 2 pounds (1 kg) veal shoulder or breast, cut into bite-size chunks
- 16 white baby onions
- 1 onion, studded with 2 cloves
- 1 medium carrot, halved
- 1 small leek, halved lengthwise
- 1 bouquet garni
- 5 cups (1.25 liters) hot chicken stock
- 2 tablespoons butter
- $\frac{1}{4}$ cup (30 g) all-purpose (plain) flour
- 12 button mushrooms
- $\frac{1}{2}$ cup (120 ml) cream
- 2 large egg yolks
- 2 tablespoons lemon juice
- Salt and freshly ground black pepper
- Fresh parsley, to garnish

Put the veal, baby onions, onion, carrot, leek, and bouquet garni in a large pan. Add the chicken stock and bring to a boil over high heat. Simmer on low, skimming frequently until the veal is tender, about 1 hour. Strain the stock, reserving the liquid. Set the veal and baby onions aside. Discard the other vegetables.

Melt the butter in a saucepan over medium heat. Add the flour and stir until the sauce is white, 1–2 minutes. Remove from the heat and whisk in $3\frac{1}{2}$ cups (870 ml) of the cooking stock. Simmer on low for 5 minutes. Add the mushrooms and simmer for 10 minutes.

Whisk the cream and egg yolks in a small bowl. Add 1 cup (250 ml) of the hot sauce. Stir the yolk mixture into the remaining sauce. Add the lemon juice and season with salt and pepper. Return the veal to the pan and gently heat through. Serve hot, garnished with parsley.

SERVES 4–6 • PREPARATION 25 MIN. • COOKING 2 HR. • LEVEL 2

14 beef bourguignon
(burgundy beef stew)

- 2 tablespoons all-purpose (plain) flour
- Salt and freshly ground black pepper
- 3 pounds (1.5 kg) stew beef, trimmed and cut into small chunks
- 4 tablespoons (60 ml) extra-virgin olive oil
- 5 ounces (150 g) bacon, finely chopped
- 8 shallots, peeled
- 1 bottle (750 ml) dry red wine
- $\frac{1}{2}$ cup (120 ml) beef stock + more as needed
- 1 clove garlic, chopped
- $\frac{1}{2}$ tablespoon fresh thyme + extra sprigs to garnish
- 2 tablespoons finely chopped fresh parsley
- 2 bay leaves
- 1 tablespoon tomato paste (concentrate)
- 8 ounces (250 g) button mushrooms, stalks removed
- Boiled potatoes or rice, to serve

Put the flour in a plastic bag and season with salt and pepper. Add the beef. Shake until well coated. Heat 1 tablespoon of oil in a large pan over medium heat. Sauté the bacon until crisp, about 5 minutes. Remove the bacon and set aside. Add the shallots to the pan and sauté over low heat until colored, 7–8 minutes. Remove the shallots and set aside. Pour the remaining oil into the pan. Sauté the beef until browned, about 5 minutes. Pour in the wine and stock and bring to a boil. Stir in the garlic, thyme, parsley, bay leaves, and tomato paste. Cover and simmer over very low heat for 1½ hours. Add more stock if the sauce dries out.

Add the bacon, shallots, and mushrooms. Simmer until the meat is very tender, about 1 more hour, stirring often. Season with salt and pepper. Garnish with thyme and serve hot with the potatoes or rice.

SERVES 6 • PREPARATION 25 MIN. • COOKING 3 HR. • LEVEL 2

15 ossobuchi alla milanese
(milan-style braised beef shanks)

Ossobuchi
- 6 veal hind shanks, cut in 1½-inch (4-cm) thick slices
- ½ cup (75 g) all-purpose (plain) flour
- Salt and freshly ground black pepper
- ¼ cup (60 ml) extra-virgin olive oil
- 3 tablespoons butter
- 1 carrot, finely chopped
- 1 onion, finely chopped
- 1 stalk celery, finely chopped
- 4 sage leaves, torn
- 1 cup (250 ml) dry white wine
- 1 cup (250 ml) beef stock
- 3 tablespoons tomatoes, peeled and diced

Gremolada (optional)
- Finely chopped zest of 1 unwaxed lemon
- 1 clove garlic, finely chopped
- 2 tablespoons finely chopped fresh parsley

Ossobuchi Make 4–5 incisions around the edge of each shank to stop them curling up during cooking. Dredge the shanks in the flour and sprinkle with salt and pepper. Heat the oil in a large, heavy-bottomed saucepan over medium-high heat and cook the shanks briefly on both sides. Remove and set aside.

Melt the butter in the pan and add the carrot, onion, celery, and sage. When the vegetables are soft, add the meat and cook for a few minutes. Pour in the wine. When the wine has evaporated, add the stock and tomatoes, and season with salt and pepper to taste.

Cover and simmer over low heat until the meat is very tender, about 1½ hours, adding extra stock if necessary.

Gremolada If serving with the gremolada, when the meat is cooked, stir in the lemon zest, garlic, and parsley. Serve hot with boiled or steamed rice or a classic Milanese risotto.

SERVES 6 • PREPARATION 25 MIN. • COOKING 2 HR. • LEVEL 2

Ossobuchi means "bones with a hole" which perfectly describes the calf's hind shank used in this classic Milanese dish. For those who like it, the bone marrow is considered a special delicacy. Gremolada, a mixture of lemon peel, garlic, and parsley, is traditionally added just before removing from the heat. It is optional.

16 pot au feu
(french boiled meats)

- 2 pounds (1 kg) beef tenderloin
- 2 pounds (1 kg) chicken
- 1 pound (500 g) lamb shoulder roast
- 4 ounces (120 g) salt pork
- 4–5 quarts (4–5 liters) water
- 1 cup (250 ml) dry white wine
- 2 cloves
- 2 medium onions
- 4 cloves garlic, finely chopped
- 3 turnips, peeled and halved
- 4 tomatoes, halved
- 6 carrots
- 2 leeks, trimmed
- 1 bouquet garni
- Salt and freshly ground black pepper
- Toast, to serve

Cover the beef, chicken, lamb, and salt pork with water in a large pot. Bring to a boil over medium heat. Pour in the wine. Press a clove into each onion and add to the pot with the garlic, turnips, tomatoes, carrots, leeks, and the bouquet garni. Season with salt and pepper. Bring to a boil and skim off any foam. Simmer over low heat until the meat is very tender, 2–3 hours.

Place the toast in individual soup bowls and ladle the stock over the top. Serve the meat and chicken, sliced, and vegetables on a large platter.

SERVES 6–8 • PREPARATION 25 MIN. • COOKING 2–3 HR. • LEVEL 1

17 bollito misto
(italian boiled meats)

- 2 medium onions, studded with 4–6 cloves
- 3 stalks celery, trimmed
- 9 large carrots, cut into chunks
- 20 black peppercorns
- 2 tablespoons coarse salt
- 4 pounds (2 kg) boneless beef (brisket, bottom round, or rump roast)
- 2 pounds (1 kg) boneless veal (breast or shoulder)
- 1 chicken, about 3 pounds (1.5 kg)
- 1 pound (500 g) calf tongue
- 1 precooked cotechino sausage, about 1$\frac{1}{2}$ pounds (750 g)
- 8 large potatoes, halved

Fill a large pot with about 6 quarts (6 liters) of cold water. Add the onions, celery, 1 carrot, peppercorns, and salt. Bring to a boil over medium-high heat. Add the beef, and when the water has returned to a boil, decrease the heat a little and cover. Simmer for 1 hour.

Add the veal, chicken, and tongue. Simmer for 1 hour, adding boiling water to cover the meats if necessary. Add the potatoes and remaining 8 carrots. Simmer until the meat and potatoes are very tender, about 1 hour.

Cook the cotechino sausage separately following the instructions on the package. Drain and serve the meats and vegetables on a large heated serving platter.

SERVES 8–10 • PREPARATION 30 MIN. • COOKING 3 HR. • LEVEL 2

18 chili con carne

- 3 tablespoons extra-virgin olive oil
- 2$\frac{1}{2}$ teaspoons chile paste
- 1 large onion, finely chopped
- 2 cloves garlic, finely chopped
- 1 long red chile, sliced
- 1 pound (500 g) ground (minced) beef
- $\frac{1}{2}$ teaspoon salt
- 2 tablespoons red wine
- 1 teaspoon red pepper flakes
- 2 teaspoons smoked paprika
- $\frac{1}{2}$ teaspoon cumin seeds
- 1 teaspoon dried oregano
- 1 teaspoon ground coriander
- 1 (4-inch/10-cm) cinnamon stick
- 1 red bell pepper (capsicum), coarsely chopped
- 2 (14-ounce/400-g) cans tomatoes, with juice
- 2 teaspoons Worcestershire sauce
- 2 tablespoons tomato purée
- 1 cup (250 ml) water
- Salt and freshly ground black pepper
- 2 (14-ounce/400-g) cans red kidney beans, drained

Heat the oil in a large saucepan over medium heat. Add 1$\frac{1}{2}$ teaspoons of chile paste and stir it into the oil for a few seconds. Add the onion and sauté until softened, 3–4 minutes. Add the garlic and chile and sauté for 2–3 minutes.

Add the beef and sauté until browned, about 5 minutes. Add the salt and wine and simmer for 2 minutes. Add the red pepper flakes, paprika, cumin, oregano, coriander, cinnamon, and bell pepper, stirring the mixture well for 1–2 minutes.

Add the tomatoes, Worcestershire sauce, and tomato purée, stirring to make a thick red sauce. Add $\frac{1}{2}$ cup (120 ml) of water. Raise the heat slightly and bring the chili to a boil, stirring all the time. Season with salt and pepper. Stir in the remaining 1 teaspoon of chile paste.

Partially cover the pan and simmer over low heat for 55–60 minutes. Stir often to stop the chili sticking to the bottom. Add the beans about 10 minutes before the end of the cooking time. Add the remaining water as required. Taste and add more salt, pepper, or chile as liked. Remove the cinnamon stick and serve hot.

SERVES 6–8 • PREPARATION 30 MIN. • COOKING 75–80 MIN.
LEVEL 2

19 beef rendang
(indonesian beef curry)

Spice Paste
- ½ cup (60 g) shredded coconut, lightly toasted
- 4 shallots, coarsely chopped
- 6 long red chiles, seeded and finely chopped
- 2 cloves garlic, chopped
- 2 teaspoons finely grated ginger
- 2 teaspoons ground coriander
- 2 teaspoons ground cumin
- 1 teaspoon ground turmeric
- 3 tablespoons vegetable oil

Curry
- 3 pounds (1.5 kg) braising steak, cut into small chunks
- 2 stalks lemongrass
- 1 cinnamon stick
- 5 cups (1.2 liters) canned coconut milk
- 1 tablespoon brown sugar
- Salt
- Freshly cooked basmati rice

Spice Paste Put all the spice paste ingredients in a large mortar and pestle or food processor and grind to make a smooth paste.

Curry Place a saucepan over medium heat. Add the spice paste and cook until fragrant, about 30 seconds. Add the beef, lemongrass, and cinnamon and sauté until coated. Add the coconut milk and sugar, and bring to a boil. Simmer on low heat, uncovered, until the liquid has evaporated, leaving the meat to fry in the oil that remains, about 2 hours. Remove the lemongrass and cinnamon and season with salt. Serve hot with rice.

SERVES 6 • PREPARATION 30 MIN. • COOKING 2 HR. • LEVEL 2

20 lamb rogan josh
(indian lamb curry)

Spice Paste
- 1/4 cup (40 g) almonds
- 2 tablespoons coriander
- 5 whole cloves
- 1/2 cinnamon stick
- 1/2 teaspoon peppercorns
- 1 tablespoon ground cumin
- 1 teaspoon chile powder
- 1 teaspoon salt
- 1/2 teaspoon ground turmeric
- 6 cloves garlic, chopped
- 1 tablespoon grated ginger
- 1/4 cup (60 ml) water

Curry
- 4 tablespoons (60 g) ghee
- 2 pounds (1 kg) stewing lamb, cut into chunks
- 1 onion, finely chopped
- 1 cup (250 ml) water
- 3/4 cup (180 g) plain yogurt
- 1/4 cup (60 g) tomato paste (concentrate)
- Cilantro (coriander)

Spice Paste Dry-fry the almonds, coriander, cloves, cinnamon, peppercorns, cumin, chile, salt, and turmeric until fragrant, about 1 minute. Transfer to a mortar and pestle or spice grinder and grind to a coarse powder. Add the garlic, ginger, and water, blending to a paste.

Curry Heat 2 tablespoons of ghee in a saucepan over high heat. Add the meat and sauté until browned, 8–10 minutes. Set aside. Heat the remaining ghee in the same pan. Sauté the onion until softened, 3–4 minutes. Stir in the spice paste. Add the water and meat, and simmer for 30 minutes. Stir in the yogurt and tomato paste, cover, and simmer until the meat is tender, about 30 minutes. Serve hot, garnished with the cilantro.

SERVES **6** • PREPARATION **30** MIN. • COOKING 1¼ HR. • LEVEL **1**

1 pork meatballs
with rice

2 chicken & coconut
meatballs

3 burgers with
onions & chutney

4 fried meatballs

5 pan-fried meatballs
with cheese filling

TOP
20

6 meat loaf
with tomato sauce

7 turkey breast
in onion sauce

8 turkey loaf
wrapped in savoy cabbage

9 chicken meat loaf

10 ground beef & beans
in baked bell peppers

11 ground beef with veggies
& mashed potatoes

12
pork sausages
with beans & tomato sauce

13
grilled sausages
with peas & garlic mash

14
grilled sausages
with apple mash

low-cost
recipes

15
beef & apple meatballs

16
sautéed calf liver
with fresh sage

17
venetian-style liver
with mash

18
meatballs in tomato sauce

19
ground beef casserole

20
sausage, pea & potato bake

1 pork meatballs
with rice

- 1 pound (500 g) ground (minced) pork
- 2 cups (120 g) fresh bread crumbs
- 2 large eggs, lightly beaten
- 2 tablespoons finely chopped fresh parsley
- 3 cloves garlic, finely chopped
- $1/3$ cup (60 g) pine nuts
- Salt and freshly ground black pepper
- $1/2$ teaspoon ground cinnamon
- $1/2$ teaspoon ground nutmeg
- $1/2$ cup (120 ml) olive oil, for frying

Place the pork in a large bowl and stir in the bread crumbs, eggs, parsley, garlic, pine nuts, salt, pepper, cinnamon, and nutmeg. Mix well.

Heat the oil in a large frying pan over medium-high heat and fry the meatballs until golden brown all over, 5–10 minutes.

Place the cooked meatballs on a plate covered with paper towels to drain. Serve hot.

SERVES 4 • PREPARATION 15 MIN. • COOKING 5–10 MIN. • LEVEL 1

2 chicken & coconut meatballs

- 1 pound (500 g) ground (minced) chicken
- ¼ cup (60 ml) Thai chile sauce + extra, to serve
- 2 cloves garlic, finely chopped
- 1 teaspoon finely chopped fresh ginger
- 1 tablespoon Thai fish sauce
- ½ cup (25 g) finely chopped fresh cilantro (coriander) + extra, to garnish
- ⅔ cup (150 ml) coconut milk
- Salt and freshly ground black pepper

Preheat the oven to 400°F (200°C/gas 6). Lightly oil two 12-cup mini muffin tins.

Combine the chicken, chile sauce, garlic, ginger, fish sauce, cilantro, and coconut milk in a medium bowl. Season with salt and pepper and mix well.

Spoon the mixture into the prepared muffin tins. Bake until golden brown and cooked through, 15–20 minutes. Serve hot with extra chile sauce.

SERVES **4** · PREPARATION **15** MIN. · COOKING **15–20** MIN. · LEVEL **1**

3 burgers
with onions & chutney

- 1¹⁄₄ pounds (600 g) ground (minced) pork or beef
- 1 large onion, finely chopped
- 1 cup (60 g) fresh bread crumbs
- 6 slices bacon, chopped
- 1 large egg, lightly beaten
- 2 cloves garlic, finely chopped
- 2 tablespoons finely chopped fresh parsely
- 1 teaspoon salt
- ¹⁄₂ teaspoon freshly ground black pepper
- 2 tablespoons extra-virgin olive oil
- 2 onions, thinly sliced
- 4 hamburger buns, halved
- ¹⁄₂ cup (120 g) chutney or ketchup
- 1 cup (50 g) mixed salad greens
- ¹⁄₂ cup (120 g) mayonnaise

Combine the meat, onion, bread crumbs, bacon, egg, garlic, parsley, salt, and pepper in a food processor and blend until just combined. Transfer the mixture to a medium bowl and shape into four even-size burgers. Place on a plate and refrigerate for 1 hour.

Preheat a grill pan or barbecue flat plate on high. Brush the burgers with 1 tablespoon of oil and grill until cooked through, about 4 minutes on each side. At the same time, drizzle the remaining 1 tablespoon of oil on the grill and cook the onions, turning frequently, until golden brown, about 5 minutes. Lightly grill the buns.

To assemble, cover the bottoms of the buns with onion, followed by the burgers, a dollop of chutney or ketchup and the salad. Smear the lids with mayonnaise and cover. Serve hot.

SERVES 4 • PREPARATION 15 MIN. + 1 HR. TO CHILL • COOKING 10–15 MIN. • LEVEL 1

Hamburgers made at home taste so much better than any you can buy. Choose a good-quality meat that is not too lean; you need a little bit of fat in the meat to stop it from becoming too dry on the grill.

4 fried meatballs

- 1 pound (500 g) ground (minced) lamb or beef
- 1 tablespoon grated fresh ginger
- 2 cloves garlic, finely chopped
- 2 fresh green chiles, seeded and finely chopped
- 1 small onion, finely chopped
- 1 large egg, lightly beaten
- 1 teaspoon ground turmeric
- 2 tablespoons finely chopped fresh cilantro (coriander)
- 4 leaves fresh mint, finely chopped + extra, to garnish
- 1 large potato, peeled and coarsely grated
- Salt
- 2 cups (500 ml) olive oil, for frying

Mix the meat, ginger, garlic, chiles, onion, egg, turmeric, cilantro, and mint in a large bowl. Stir in the grated potato. Season with salt. Shape the mixture into balls about the size of a golf ball. Chill in the refrigerator for 30 minutes.

Heat the oil in a large, deep frying pan to very hot. Fry the meatballs in batches for 8–10 minutes, until browned all over. Drain well on paper towels. Garnish with the mint leaves and serve hot.

SERVES 4–6 • PREPARATION 15 MIN. + 30 MIN. TO REST • COOKING 15–20 MIN. • LEVEL 1

5 pan-fried meatballs
with cheese filling

- 2 cups (120 g) fresh bread crumbs
- $\frac{1}{4}$ cup (60 ml) milk
- $1\frac{1}{2}$ pounds (750 g) lean ground (minced) beef
- 1 large egg, lightly beaten
- 2 tablespoons finely chopped fresh parsley
- Salt and freshly ground black pepper
- 6 ounces (180 g) mild firm cheese, cut into small cubes
- $\frac{1}{4}$ cup (30 g) all-purpose (plain) flour
- $\frac{1}{4}$ cup (60 g) butter
- $\frac{1}{2}$ cup (120 ml) dry white wine

Drizzle the bread crumbs with the milk in a small bowl. Combine the meat with the bread crumbs, egg, and parsley in a large bowl. Season with salt and pepper. Shape into meatballs. Push a piece of cheese into the center of each one, sealing the meat around it.

Put the flour on a plate and dredge the meatballs in it. Melt the butter in a large saucepan over medium heat. Add the meatballs and sauté until browned all over, about 5 minutes. Add the wine and simmer for 2–3 minutes. Lower the heat, cover, and simmer until the meatballs are tender and cooked through, 15–20 minutes. Serve hot or at room temperature.

SERVES 4 • PREPARATION 15 MIN. • COOKING 25–30 MIN • LEVEL 1

6 meat loaf
with tomato sauce

- 1¹/₂ pounds (750 g) ground (minced) beef
- 1 large egg
- 8 ounces (250 g) highly flavored pork sausage, crumbled
- Dash of nutmeg
- 1 cup (60 g) fresh bread crumbs bread, soaked in 2 tablespoons milk and squeezed dry
- 1 clove garlic, finely chopped
- 2 tablespoons finely chopped fresh parsley + extra, to garnish
- Salt and freshly ground black pepper
- ¹/₄ cup (30 g) all-purpose (plain) flour
- ¹/₂ cup (120 ml) extra-virgin olive oil
- 1 tablespoon butter
- 1 small onion, finely chopped
- 1 small carrot, finely chopped
- 1 small stalk celery, finely chopped
- 2 cups (500 g) peeled and chopped fresh or canned tomatoes
- 1 cup (250 ml) beef stock, if required
- Garlic mash, to serve (see page 285)

Mix the beef with the egg, sausage, nutmeg, bread, garlic, and parsley in a bowl. Season with salt and pepper. Shape the mixture into a meat loaf. Put the flour in a large dish and carefully roll the meat loaf in it.

Heat ¹/₄ cup (60 ml) of oil in a large, heavy-bottomed pan over medium heat and carefully brown the meat loaf all over, about 10 minutes. Use a wooden fork and spatula when turning, taking care that the loaf doesn't crumble or break up. Drain the meat loaf of the cooking oil and set aside.

Heat the butter and the remaining ¹/₄ cup (60 ml) of oil in a sauté pan. Add the onion, carrot, and celery and sauté for 4–5 minutes. Add the tomatoes and simmer for 5 minutes. Return the meat loaf to the pan and season with salt and pepper. Partially cover the pan and simmer over low heat for about 1 hour. Stir frequently, so that the meat loaf does not stick to the bottom. If the sauce becomes too dense, add some of the stock.

Set aside to cool. Slice the tepid meat loaf and arrange on a serving dish. Heat the sauce just before serving and pour over the slices. Serve with the garlic mash.

SERVES 4–6 • PREPARATION 30 MIN. + 1 HR. TO COOL • COOKING 1¹/₂ HR. • LEVEL 2

7 turkey breast
in onion sauce

- 3 pounds (1.5 kg) turkey breast
- Salt and freshly ground black pepper
- 3 tablespoons all-purpose (plain) flour
- $\frac{1}{2}$ cup (120 ml) extra-virgin olive oil
- 1 tablespoon butter
- 4 large white onions, coarsely sliced
- 4 cups (1 liter) beef stock
- Mashed potato, to serve

Roll the turkey breast and tie with kitchen string. Season with salt and pepper and dredge in the flour. Transfer to a heavy-bottomed pan with the oil and butter and sauté over high heat for 5–7 minutes. Add the onions, stirring carefully and making sure the turkey is always touching the bottom of the pan (rather than on the onions). Sauté for 5 minutes more.

Pour in enough stock to almost cover the meat. Partially cover the pan, decrease the heat to low, and simmer until the meat is cooked and the onions have melted to form a creamy sauce, about 45 minutes. Serve hot with the mashed potatoes.

SERVES 6–8 • PREPARATION 15 MIN. • COOKING 1 HR. • LEVEL 2

8 turkey loaf
wrapped in savoy cabbage

- 1½ pounds (750 g) ground (minced) turkey breast
- 5 ounces (150 g) pork sausages, crumbled
- ½ cup (60 g) bacon, chopped
- ½ cup (60 g) freshly grated Parmesan cheese
- 1 large egg + 1 large yolk
- 1 cup (60 g) fresh bread crumbs soaked in hot milk and well squeezed
- Dash of nutmeg
- Salt and freshly ground black pepper
- 8–10 leaves Savoy cabbage
- 2 shallots, sliced
- 2 cups (500 g) tomatoes, peeled and chopped
- ⅓ cup (90 ml) extra-virgin olive oil
- ½ cup (120 ml) white wine
- ½ cup (120 ml) beef stock

Preheat the oven to 400°F (200°C/gas 6). Combine the turkey, sausage, bacon, Parmesan, eggs, bread crumbs, nutmeg, salt, and pepper in a large bowl and mix well.

Parboil the cabbage leaves in salted water for 4–5 minutes. Drain well. Arrange the leaves on a work surface to form a rectangle; they should be overlapping. Place the turkey mixture in the middle and shape into a meat loaf. Wrap the leaves around the turkey, taking care not to tear them. Tie with kitchen string.

Transfer the turkey loaf to an ovenproof dish with the shallots, tomatoes, and oil. Bake for 1¼ hours, basting frequently with the wine. When all the wine has been added, continue basting with the stock. Serve hot.

SERVES 4 • PREPARATION 45 MIN. • COOKING 1½ HR. • LEVEL 2

9 chicken meat loaf

- 1½ pounds (750 g) ground (minced) chicken breast
- 2 cups (120 g) fresh bread crumbs
- ½ cup (100 g) canned corn (sweet corn), drained
- 1 cup (150 g) frozen peas
- 1 large egg
- Salt and freshly ground black pepper
- ¼ cup (60 ml) extra-virgin olive oil

Preheat the oven to 350°F (180°C/gas 4). Place the chicken breast, bread crumbs, corn, peas, egg, salt, and pepper in a bowl and mix well.

Shape the chicken mixture into a meat loaf and wrap in damp parchment paper. Tie with kitchen string. Place in a baking dish and drizzle with the oil.

Bake until tender and cooked through, about 45 minutes. Unwrap and discard the paper. Cut in slices and serve hot. Alternatively, let cool and serve at room temperature.

SERVES 4–6 • PREPARATION 15 MIN. • COOKING 45 MIN. • LEVEL 1

If liked, add a teaspoon of dried oregano to the mixture. Serve the loaf warm or at room temperature. It makes a great picnic dish and is also good sliced in sandwiches.

10 ground beef & beans
in baked bell peppers

- 4 red bell peppers (capsicums), halved and seeded
- 1 pound (500 g) ground (minced) beef
- 1 onion, finely chopped
- 2 tablespoons extra-virgin olive oil
- 2 teaspoons chile powder
- 1 (14-ounce/400-g) can tomatoes, with juice
- Salt and freshly ground black pepper
- 1 (14-ounce/400-g) can white kidney beans, drained
- Sour cream, to serve
- Fresh cilantro (coriander) leaves, to garnish

Preheat the oven to 400°F (200°C/gas 6). Arrange the bell peppers skin-side down in a roasting pan. Bake for 25–30 minutes, until softened.

Sauté the beef and onion in the oil in a large frying pan over medium heat for 5 minutes. Add the chile powder and tomatoes. Season with salt and pepper. Bring to a boil then simmer over low heat until reduced, 15 minutes. Add the beans and stir until heated through.

Spoon the beef mixture into the bell peppers. Top with sour cream and garnish with the cilantro. Serve hot.

SERVES 4 • PREPARATION 15 MIN. • COOKING 25–30 MIN. • LEVEL 1

11 ground beef with veggies
& mashed potatoes

- 1 pound (500 g) potatoes, peeled and diced
- 2 tablespoons butter
- 2 tablespoons milk
- Salt and freshly ground black pepper
- 1 onion, finely chopped
- 2 cloves garlic, finely chopped
- 1 tablespoon extra-virgin olive oil
- 1 pound (500 g) ground (minced) beef
- 2 cups (500 g) chopped tomatoes
- 1 cup (150 g) frozen mixed peas, carrots, and corn
- Sprigs of parsley, to garnish

Cook the potatoes in a boiling water until tender, 10 minutes. Drain and return to the pan. Add the butter and milk. Mash until smooth. Season with salt and pepper.

Sauté the onion and garlic in the oil in a large frying pan over medium heat until softened, 3–4 minutes. Add the beef and sauté until browned, about 5 minutes. Stir in the tomatoes. Bring to a boil, cover, and simmer over low heat until reduced, 10–15 minutes. Add the vegetables and simmer for 10 minutes. Season with salt and pepper. Serve hot with the potatoes and parsley.

SERVES 4 • PREPARATION 20 MIN. • COOKING 25–30 MIN. • LEVEL 1

12 pork sausages
with beans & tomato sauce

- ¹/₄ cup (60 ml) extra-virgin olive oil
- 2 cloves garlic, chopped
- 4 leaves sage
- 1 (14-ounce/400-g) can cannellini or white kidney beans, drained
- 1 pound (500 g) tomatoes, peeled and diced
- Salt and freshly ground black pepper
- 8 highly-flavored pork sausages

Heat the oil in a heavy-bottomed pan, preferably earthenware, and sauté the garlic and sage until softened, 3–4 minutes. Add the beans and cook for a few minutes so that they absorb the seasoning.

Add the tomatoes and season with salt and pepper. Prick the sausages with a fork and add to the beans. Cover and cook over medium-low heat for about 25 minutes, stirring frequently. Serve hot.

SERVES 4 • PREPARATION 15 MIN. • COOKING 25–30 MIN. • LEVEL 1

This recipe is based on an old Tuscan dish. If you have the time, use dried beans that have been soaked for 12 hours and then cooked in salted water until tender.

13 grilled sausages
with peas & garlic mash

- 2 pounds (1 kg) potatoes, peeled
- 2 cloves garlic, finely chopped
- $1/4$ cup (60 g) salted butter
- 2 cups (300 g) frozen peas
- 8 medium sausages
- 8 cloves garlic, whole

Boil the potatoes in a saucepan of salted water until tender, 20–25 minutes. Drain well and mash with the garlic and butter. Cook the peas in salted boiling water until tender, about 5 minutes. Drain well.

Preheat a grill pan or barbecue flat plate. Grill the sausages with the whole cloves of garlic until golden brown and cooked, 5–10 minutes. Serve hot with the garlic mash and peas.

SERVES 4 · PREPARATION 15 MIN. · COOKING 20–30 MIN. · LEVEL 1

14 grilled sausages
with apple mash

- 2 pounds (1 kg) potatoes, peeled and diced
- 2 medium tart apples, peeled and quartered
- $\frac{1}{2}$ teaspoon salt
- $\frac{1}{4}$ cup (60 g) butter
- 1 small onion, quartered and thinly sliced
- 1 teaspoon cider vinegar
- $\frac{1}{2}$ teaspoon sugar
- Dash of ground nutmeg
- 8 medium sausages
- Fresh chives, to garnish

Put the potatoes, apples, and salt in a large saucepan; add enough water to cover. Bring to a boil, cover, and simmer for 10 minutes, until tender. Melt the butter in a small frying pan over medium heat. Add the onion and sauté until softened, 3–4 minutes. Drain the potatoes and apples. Add the butter and onion mixture, vinegar, sugar, and nutmeg and mash until smooth.

Preheat a grill pan or barbecue flat plate. Grill the sausages until golden brown and cooked, 5–10 minutes. Serve hot with the apple mash, garnished with chives.

SERVES 4 • PREPARATION 15 MIN. • COOKING 15–20 MIN. • LEVEL 1

15 beef & apple meatballs

- 2 medium apples (Granny Smiths are ideal), grated
- 1¼ pounds (600 g) finely ground (minced) lean beef
- 2 large eggs, beaten
- ½ cup (60 g) freshly grated Parmesan cheese
- 2 cloves garlic, finely chopped
- Salt and freshly ground black pepper
- 1 cup (150 g) all-purpose (plain) flour
- ½ cup (120 g) butter
- ¼ cup (60 ml) dry white wine
- 2 tablespoons sugar

Put the apples in a medium bowl with the beef, eggs, Parmesan, garlic, salt, and pepper and mix well. Form tablespoons of the mixture into oblong croquettes and dredge in the flour.

Heat the butter in a large frying pan over medium-high heat and fry the croquettes until golden brown all over, 8–10 minutes.

Heat the wine in a small saucepan over low heat. Add the sugar and stir until dissolved. Drizzle spoonfuls of the wine mixture over the croquettes. Simmer until reduced a little. Serve hot or at room temperature.

SERVES 4 • PREPARATION 20 MIN. • COOKING 10–15 MIN. • LEVEL 1

The apples add a smooth texture and a sweet, fresh flavor to these meatballs.

16 sautéed calf liver
with fresh sage

- 1¼ pounds (600 g) calf liver, sliced
- 2 heaped tablespoons all-purpose (plain) flour
- 2 tablespoons extra-virgin olive oil
- 2 cloves garlic, finely chopped
- 10 leaves fresh sage
- Salt and freshly ground black pepper
- Mashed potatoes, to serve
- Green salad, to serve

Ask your butcher to slice the liver ready for cooking. Lightly flour the liver and set aside on a plate.

Heat the oil in a large, heavy-bottomed pan and add the garlic and sage. Sauté over medium-high heat for 1–2 minutes, then add the liver.

Cook until well-browned on both sides, 5–8 minutes. Serve hot with the mashed potatoes and green salad.

SERVES 4 • PREPARATION 10 MIN. • COOKING 7–10 MIN. • LEVEL 1

17 venetian-style liver
with mash

- 1¹/₂ pounds (750 g) white onions, thinly sliced
- ¹/₄ cup (60 g) butter
- 2 tablespoons extra-virgin olive oil
- 1¹/₂ pounds (750 g) calf liver, cut into thin strips
- Salt and freshly ground black pepper
- 2 tablespoons finely chopped fresh parsley
- Mashed potatoes, to serve

Place the onions, butter, and oil in a large frying pan over low heat. Let sweat gently for 20 minutes, then add the liver.

Cook over high heat, stirring and turning constantly for 5 minutes at most (or the liver will become tough). Sprinkle with salt just before removing from the heat.

Season with pepper, sprinkle with the parsley, and serve hot with the mashed potatoes.

SERVES 6 • PREPARATION 15 MIN. • COOKING 25–30 MIN. • LEVEL 1

18 meatballs in tomato sauce

Sauce
- 3 tablespoons extra-virgin olive oil
- 1 small white onion, finely chopped
- 14 ounces (400 g) fresh or canned tomatoes, peeled and chopped
- 1 teaspoon oregano
- Salt

Meatballs
- 1 cup (60 g) fresh bread crumbs
- 1/4 cup (60 ml) milk
- 1 pound (500 g) ground (minced) beef
- Scant 1 cup (100 g) freshly grated pecorino or other firm, tasty cheese
- 2 large eggs, lightly beaten
- 1/2 small onion, finely chopped
- 1 tablespoon finely chopped fresh parsley + extra, to garnish
- 1 clove garlic, finely chopped
- Salt and freshly ground black pepper
- Rice or potatoes, to serve

Sauce Heat the oil in a large, heavy-bottomed saucepan over medium heat. Add the onion and sauté until softened, 3–4 minutes. Add the tomatoes, oregano, and salt. Cook, uncovered, over medium-low heat until reduced a little, about 10 minutes.

Meatballs Place the bread crumbs in a large bowl with the milk. Stir in the beef, cheese, eggs, onion, parsley, and garlic. Season with salt and pepper and mix thoroughly.

Shape the mixture into small meatballs and add to the hot tomato sauce. Simmer for 15–20 minutes, turning carefully once or twice. Serve hot, garnished with extra parsley, with the rice or potatoes.

SERVES 4 • PREPARATION 15 MIN. • COOKING 25–30 MIN. • LEVEL 2

Children will love these meatballs. Serve them with mashed potatoes or rice and a green salad for a nutritious family meal.

19 ground beef casserole

- 1½ pounds (750 g) lean ground (minced) beef
- 2 cloves garlic, finely sliced
- 1 tablespoon finely chopped fresh parsley
- ½ teaspoon salt
- ½ teaspoon freshly ground white pepper
- 1½ pounds (750 g) potatoes, cut in small cubes
- 2 large onions, thinly sliced
- 1 large carrot, diced
- 8 ounces (250 g) white mushrooms, thinly sliced
- 1 cup (150 g) frozen peas
- 3 tablespoons all-purpose (plain) flour
- ½ cup (120 ml) milk
- 1 tablespoon Worcestershire sauce

Preheat the oven to 350°F (180°C/gas 4). Stir together the beef, garlic, parsley, salt, and pepper in a Dutch oven or casserole dish. Add the potatoes, onions, carrot, mushrooms, and peas.

Combine the flour in a small bowl with the milk and stir until smooth. Pour the milk mixture and Worcestershire sauce in over the top and mix gently.

Bake until the meat and potatoes are tender, 45–60 minutes. Stir several times during cooking. Serve hot.

SERVES 4–6 • PREPARATION 15 MIN. • COOKING 45–60 MIN. • LEVEL 1

20 sausage, pea & potato bake

- 1½ pounds (750 g) pork sausages, sliced
- 4 large potatoes, peeled and cubed
- 2 cups (300 g) frozen peas
- 4 cloves garlic, finely chopped
- 2 cups (500 ml) milk
- 1 (10-ounce/300-g) can cream of mushroom soup
- Salt and freshly ground black pepper

Preheat the oven to 350°F (180°C/gas 4). Combine the sausages, potatoes, peas, garlic, milk, and soup in a large casserole dish. Season with salt and pepper and stir gently until well mixed.

Cover the dish and bake until the potatoes are tender, about 1½ hours. Serve hot.

SERVES **4–6** • PREPARATION **20** MIN. • COOKING 1½ HR. • LEVEL **1**

1

beef & stout
stew

2

beef & beer
stew

3

chicken casserole
with red wine & dumplings

4

cardamom lamb curry
with almonds

5

scotch beef
with dried fruit

TOP
20

6

beef & red wine casserole

7

lamb stew
with lemon & garlic

8

lamb stew
with beans, olives & risoni

9

tuscan-style braised beef

10

beef & veggie stew

11

farmhouse stew

12

lamb stew
with rosemary, garlic & peas

13

slow-roasted spiced lamb

14

braised beef in barolo

long & slow
recipes

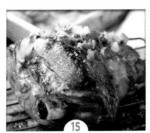

15

roast leg of lamb
with aromatic herbs

16

chicken tagine
with pears & cinnamon

17

lamb tagine
with raisins, honey & almonds

18

roasted veal roll
with potatoes

19

venison casserole

20

lamb & potato casserole

1 beef & stout stew

- 2 tablespoons vegetable oil
- 2 pounds (1 kg) beef chuck roast, cut into small chunks
- ½ teaspoon salt
- ½ teaspoon freshly ground black pepper
- ¼ teaspoon dried rosemary
- ¼ teaspoon dried sage
- ¼ teaspoon dried tarragon
- 1 bay leaf
- 1¼ cups (300 ml) beef stock
- 1¼ cups (300 ml) stout beer
- 4 carrots, diced
- 4 potatoes, peeled and diced
- 6 onions, quartered
- ¼ cup (30 g) all-purpose (plain) flour
- ¼ cup (60 ml) water

Heat the oil in a large saucepan over high heat. Add the beef and sauté until browned all over, about 10 minutes. Add the salt, pepper, rosemary, sage, tarragon, and bay leaf. Pour in the beef stock and stout. Cover and simmer for about 2 hours.

Add the carrots, potatoes, and onions and continue cooking until the vegetables are tender, 30–40 minutes.

Mix the flour and water in a small bowl until smooth. Stir into the stew and simmer until it has thickened slightly. Discard the bay leaf and serve hot.

SERVES 4–6 • PREPARATION 20 MIN. • COOKING 3 HR. • LEVEL 1

2 beef & beer stew

- 3 pounds (1.5 kg) beef chuck roast, cut into chunks
- Salt and freshly ground black pepper
- 3 bay leaves
- 3 sprigs thyme
- 3 sprigs rosemary
- ¼ cup (60 ml) vegetable oil
- 2 tablespoons butter
- 2 large white onions, chopped
- ⅓ cup (50 g) all-purpose (plain) flour
- 1 (12-ounce/350 ml) bottle dark beer
- 4 cups (1 liter) hot beef stock
- 1 (14-ounce/400-g) can tomatoes, with juice
- 4 potatoes, peeled and diced
- 3 carrots, diced
- 3 stalks celery, finely sliced
- 1 small rutabaga (swede), peeled and diced

Season the beef with salt and pepper. Tie the bay leaves, thyme, and rosemary to make a bouquet garni.

Heat the oil and butter in a saucepan over high heat. Add the beef and sauté until browned, about 10 minutes. Set aside. Add the onions to the pan and sauté over medium heat until softened, 3–4 minutes. Simmer on low until golden and caramelized, about 45 minutes.

Sprinkle the onions with the flour and stir. Return the beef to the pan. Add the beer, stock, tomatoes, and bouquet garni. Season with salt and pepper. Bring to a boil, cover, and simmer for 45 minutes. Add the vegetables and simmer for 1 hour. Serve hot.

SERVES 4–6 • PREPARATION 30 MIN. • COOKING 2¾ HR. • LEVEL 2

3 chicken casserole
with red wine & dumplings

Casserole
- 6 large chicken pieces
- Salt and freshly ground black pepper
- 3 tablespoons all-purpose (plain) flour
- 3 tablespoons extra-virgin olive oil
- 3 onions, peeled and cut into wedges
- 8 ounces (250 g) pancetta or bacon pieces
- 3 cloves garlic, thinly sliced
- 12 ounces (350 g) large flat mushrooms, sliced
- 2 bay leaves
- 6 strips peeled unwaxed orange zest
- 1 cup (250 ml) red wine
- 1 1/2 cups (370 ml) chicken stock

Dumplings
- 2/3 cup (100 g) all-purpose (plain)
- 1 teaspoon baking powder
- 1 3/4 cups (100 g) fresh white bread crumbs
- 1 tablespoon Dijon mustard
- 2/3 cup (150 g) butter, cubed
- 2 teaspoons fresh thyme leaves
- 2 tablespoons fresh parsley, chopped
- 2 large eggs, lightly beaten
- Salt and freshly ground black pepper

Casserole Preheat the oven to 325°F (170°C/gas 3). Season the chicken with salt and pepper and dust with 2 tablespoons of the flour. Heat the oil in a large Dutch oven and brown the chicken all over on high heat, 5–10 minutes. Set the chicken aside.

Add the onions and pancetta and sauté over medium heat until browned, about 5 minutes. Add the garlic and remaining tablespoon of flour and cook for 1 minute, stirring to prevent sticking.

Add the mushrooms, bay leaves, orange zest, wine, and chicken stock and season with salt and pepper. Return the chicken to the pan, making sure it is well covered with the liquid, and bring to a boil. Cover and bake in the oven for 1 hour.

Dumplings Put the flour, baking powder, bread crumbs, mustard, and butter in a food processor and blend until crumbly. Add the thyme, parsley, eggs, salt, and pepper. Blend again to form a fairly moist dough. Using floured hands, roll the dough into 6 large, even-size balls.

Remove the casserole from the oven after 1 hour and sit the dumplings on top. Cover again and bake for 45 more minutes, until the chicken is very tender and the dumplings have puffed up. Serve hot.

SERVES 6 • PREPARATION 30 MIN. • COOKING 2 HR. • LEVEL 2

4 cardamom lamb curry
with almonds

Curry Paste
- 2 cloves garlic, finely chopped
- 2 green chiles, finely chopped
- 1 onion, finely chopped
- $\frac{1}{2}$ teaspoon salt
- 1 teaspoon ground cardamom
- 1 teaspoon water

Lamb Curry
- $1\frac{1}{2}$ tablespoons butter
- 1 tablespoon sunflower oil
- 4 cardamom pods, crushed
- 1 small cinnamon stick
- $1\frac{1}{2}$ pounds (750 g) leg of lamb, cut into small cubes
- Salt
- 3 tablespoons plain yogurt
- Water as needed
- $\frac{2}{3}$ cup (150 ml) cream
- Freshly ground white pepper
- 1 tablespoon fresh cilantro (coriander) leaves
- 1 tablespoon flaked almonds, toasted

Curry Paste Pound the garlic with the chiles, onion, and salt with a mortar and pestle. Mix in the cardamom and water to make a smooth paste. Set aside.

Lamb Curry Heat the butter and oil in a large saucepan over medium heat. Add the cardamom pods and cinnamon stick and stir for 10 seconds to release their flavor. Add the curry paste and sauté for 5 minutes.

Add the lamb and sauté until browned, 8–10 minutes. Season with salt. Stir in the yogurt and enough water to just cover the meat. Cover the pan. Simmer over low heat for 1–2 hours. Uncover and cook for 15 minutes, until the sauce is well reduced. Pour in the cream. Bring to a boil, and season with salt and white pepper. Garnish with cilantro and flaked almonds. Serve hot.

SERVES 4 • PREPARATION 30 MIN. • COOKING $1\frac{1}{2}$–$2\frac{1}{2}$ HR. • LEVEL 1

5 scotch beef
with dried fruit

- 1 cup (250 g) pitted prunes
- 6 ounces (180 g) dried apricots
- Water
- 3 pounds (1.5 kg) beef silverside or brisket
- Salt and freshly ground black pepper
- 2 tablespoons butter
- 2 onions, thinly sliced
- 1 large apple, thinly sliced
- 1 tablespoon brown sugar
- 1 teaspoon crushed cloves
- 1/2 cup (120 ml) whiskey
- 1 bay leaf
- 1 tablespoon all-purpose (plain) flour
- 2 tablespoons finely chopped fresh parsley

Soak the prunes and apricots in cold water overnight. Drain, reserving the water. Season the beef with salt and pepper. Melt the butter in a large saucepan over high heat. Brown the beef all over, 8–10 minutes.

Add the onions, apple, sugar, cloves, whiskey, 1 cup (250 ml) water, and bay leaf and bring to a boil. Cover and simmer over low heat for 2 hours. Add the prunes, apricots, and 1/2 cup (120 ml) of soaking liquid. Cook for 30 minutes. Season with salt and pepper. Slice the meat and transfer to a serving dish with the fruit.

Blend the flour with a little water. Stir into the cooking juices. Cook for 2 minutes, stirring constantly. Spoon over the meat. Garnish with the parsley and serve hot.

SERVES 4 • PREPARATION 20 MIN. + 12 HR. TO SOAK • COOKING 2 3/4 HR. • LEVEL 1

6 beef & red wine casserole

- 3 tablespoons all-purpose (plain) flour
- Salt and freshly ground black pepper
- 1¼ pounds (600 g) beef (braising or chuck steak), cut into cubes
- 2 tablespoons extra-virgin olive oil
- 2 onions, coarsely chopped
- 2 sprigs thyme
- 1 cup (250 ml) dry red wine
- 1¼ cups (300 ml) beef stock
- 2 carrots, sliced
- 8 ounces (250 g) cooked, peeled chestnuts, freshly roasted or vacuum packed
- Freshly cooked rice or potatoes, to serve

Season the flour generously with salt and pepper. Sprinkle over the beef, turning to coat. Heat the oil in a deep saucepan over high heat. Add the beef and sauté until browned, 8–10 minutes.

Add the onions and sauté until they start to brown, 4–5 minutes. Add the thyme, wine, and stock. Bring to a boil, then decrease the heat, cover, and simmer for 1 hour.

Add the carrots and chestnuts, season with salt and pepper, and simmer until the meat is very tender, about 1 more hour.

Serve hot with rice or potatoes.

SERVES **4** • PREPARATION **20** MIN. • COOKING **2¼** HR. • LEVEL **1**

Whole, cooked vacuum-packed chestnuts are available in many supermarkets and delicatessens. You can also prepare your own chestnuts by soaking them in water for 30 minutes, then roasting them. Pierce the soaked chestnut skins with a sharp knife then roast at 425°F (225°C/gas 7) for 30 minutes. Let cool a little, then peel.

7 lamb stew
with lemon & garlic

- 3 tablespoons extra-virgin olive oil
- 2 pounds (1 kg) lean boneless lamb, diced
- 1 onion, finely chopped
- 3 cloves garlic, finely chopped
- 1 tablespoon hot paprika
- 3 tablespoons coarsely chopped fresh parsley + extra, to garnish
- 3 tablespoons freshly squeezed lemon juice
- Salt and freshly ground black pepper
- $\frac{1}{2}$ cup (120 ml) dry white wine or water, as needed
- Freshly cooked couscous, to serve

Heat the oil in a large frying pan over medium heat. Add the lamb and sauté until browned, 5–10 minutes. Set the lamb aside.

Add the onion and garlic to the pan and sauté over medium heat until softened, 3–4 minutes. Stir in the paprika, lamb (and any cooking juices), parsley, and lemon juice. Season with salt and pepper. Cover and simmer over very low heat, stirring occasionally, until the lamb is very tender, about 1¾ hours. Add the wine or water gradually during cooking. Serve hot with the couscous and extra parsley.

SERVES 4–6 • PREPARATION 15 MIN. • COOKING 2 HR. • LEVEL 1

8 lamb stew
with beans, olives & risoni

- 4 lamb shanks
- 2 cloves garlic, finely chopped
- 1 onion, finely chopped
- 2 tablespoons extra-virgin olive oil
- 2 cups (500 ml) beef stock
- 4 sprigs fresh oregano
- 2 tablespoons tomato paste (concentrate)
- 2 cups (500 ml) water
- 4 ounces (120 g) risoni (orzo)
- 1 cup (200 g) canned butter beans or lima beans, drained
- 1/2 cup (50 g) black olives
- 2 teaspoons finely chopped fresh oregano
- Salt and freshly ground black pepper

Brown the lamb shanks with the garlic and onion in the oil in a large saucepan over medium heat for 5 minutes. Add the beef stock, oregano, tomato paste, and 1 cup (250 ml) of water. Bring to a boil. Decrease the heat, cover, and simmer until tender and cooked through, about 1½ hours. Remove the shanks from the pan and slice the meat off the bone. Set aside.

Add the risoni and the remaining 1 cup (250 ml) of water. Cook the risoni until al dente, about 5 minutes. Add the beans, olives, lamb, and oregano. Season with salt and pepper. Cook for 5 minutes. Serve hot.

SERVES 4–6 • PREPARATION 15 MIN. • COOKING 2 HR. • LEVEL 2

9 tuscan-style braised beef

- 1 clove garlic, finely chopped
- 1 tablespoon rosemary, finely chopped
- Salt and freshly ground black pepper
- 2 pounds (1 kg) beef chuck
- 1/3 cup (90 ml) extra-virgin olive oil
- 2 onions, coarsely chopped
- 2 carrots, coarsely chopped
- 1 stalk celery, coarsely chopped
- 1 tablespoon parsley, finely chopped
- 3 leaves sage, torn
- 2 bay leaves
- 1 cup (250 ml) dry red wine
- 2 cups (500 g) tomatoes, peeled and chopped
- 2 cups (500 ml) beef stock
- Sliced boiled potatoes or rice, to serve

Mix the garlic and rosemary with a generous quantity of salt and pepper. Using a sharp knife, make several incisions in the meat and fill with the herb mixture. Tie the meat loosely with kitchen string.

Heat the oil in a heavy-bottomed pan over medium-high heat and brown the meat well on all sides, 8–10 minutes. Add the onions, carrots, celery, parsley, sage, and bay leaves and sauté for 5 minutes.

Season with salt and pepper, then pour in the wine. When the wine has evaporated, add the tomatoes, partially cover and simmer over medium-low heat for about 2½ hours. Turn the meat from time to time, adding the stock gradually so that the sauce doesn't dry out. When the meat is cooked, transfer to a heated serving dish and cut in slices. Spoon the sauce and cooking juices over the top, and serve hot.

SERVES 4–6 • PREPARATION 20 MIN. • COOKING 3 HR. • LEVEL 2

In this traditional Tuscan recipe, the beef is braised slowly in red wine and stock. After 3 hours the meat is extremely tender. If there is any braised beef left over, chop the meat finely, mix with the sauce and serve the next day with fresh pasta, such as tagliatelle or tortelloni.

10 beef & veggie stew

- 3 tablespoons vegetable oil
- 1 onion, diced
- 1 carrot, diced
- 1 leek, diced
- 2 stalks celery, diced
- 2 cloves garlic, crushed
- 3 ounces (90 g) mushrooms, sliced
- 1½ pounds (750 g) braising steak, cubed
- 2 tablespoons all-purpose (plain) flour
- 3 sprigs of thyme
- 3 cups (750 ml) beef stock
- 2 tablespoons tomato paste (concentrate)
- Dash of Worcestershire sauce
- Salt and freshly ground black pepper
- 4 large potatoes, quartered

Heat 2 tablespoons of oil in a large pan over medium heat. Add the onion, carrot, leek, celery and garlic, and simmer for 5 minutes, without browning. Add the mushrooms and simmer for 5 more minutes, then remove from the pan.

Heat the remaining 1 tablespoon of oil in the pan over high heat. Add the beef and brown all over, 5–10 minutes. Stir the flour in well. Return the vegetables to the pan and add the thyme, stock, tomato paste, and Worcestershire sauce. Season with salt and pepper. Cover and simmer until tender, about 2 hours. Add the potatoes to the pan after about 1 hour. Serve hot.

SERVES **4–6** · PREPARATION **15** MIN. · COOKING **2**¼ HR. · LEVEL **2**

11 farmhouse stew

- $1/3$ cup (90 ml) extra-virgin olive oil
- 2 cloves garlic, 1 onion, 1 carrot, 1 stalk celery, all finely chopped
- 4 medium tomatoes, peeled and chopped
- 1 tablespoon mixed herbs (sage, parsley, oregano, rosemary, thyme), chopped
- $1^{1}/_{2}$ pounds (750 g) beef chuck with muscle, cut into bite-size pieces
- Salt and freshly ground black pepper
- 1 cup (250 ml) red wine
- 2 cups (500 ml) beef stock
- $1^{1}/_{4}$ pounds (600 g) potatoes, peeled and cut in bite-size chunks

Heat the oil in a large, heavy-bottomed pan over medium heat. Add the chopped vegetables and herbs. Sauté until softened, about 5 minutes.

Remove any little pieces of fat from the meat. Add the meat to the pan, season with salt and pepper, and cook until brown. Pour in the wine and cook until it evaporates. Cover the pan and simmer for about 2 hours, gradually adding the stock. Stir frequently, to stop the meat from sticking to the pan. Add the potatoes and simmer until tender, 30–45 minutes. Serve hot.

SERVES **4–6** • PREPARATION **15 MIN.** • COOKING **2$^{3}/_{4}$ HR.** • LEVEL **1**

12 lamb stew
with rosemary, garlic & peas

- ⅓ cup (90 ml) extra-virgin olive oil
- 2 cloves garlic, finely chopped
- 1 tablespoon rosemary, finely chopped + extra, to garnish
- ½ cup (60 g) diced pancetta
- 2½ pounds (1.2 kg) lamb shoulder, cut into pieces, with bone
- Salt and freshly ground black pepper
- ½ cup (120 ml) dry white wine
- 3 large tomatoes, peeled and coarsely chopped
- 3½ cups (500 g) fresh or frozen peas
- Boiled rice, to serve

Heat the oil in a large saucepan over medium heat. Add the garlic, rosemary, and pancetta and sauté until the garlic and pancetta are pale golden brown, 4–5 minutes. Add the lamb, season with salt and pepper, and sauté until lightly browned, 8–10 minutes.

Pour in the wine and cook until it has evaporated. Stir in the tomatoes, decrease the heat to low, and partially cover the pan. Simmer until the lamb is very tender, about 2 hours. Add the peas to the pan about 45 minutes before the meat is cooked.

Serve the stew hot garnished with the rosemary over the rice.

SERVES 6 • PREPARATION 15 MIN. • COOKING 2 HR. • LEVEL 2

Add some color to the stew by reserving ½ cup of peas to add 5 minutes before the stew is cooked.

13 slow-roasted spiced lamb

- 1 leg of lamb, bone in, about 5 pounds (2.5 kg)
- ²/₃ cup (150 g) butter, softened
- 2 cloves garlic, finely chopped
- 1½ tablespoons hot paprika
- 1 tablespoon ground cumin
- 2 teaspoons ground coriander
- 1 teaspoon ground cinnamon
- 1 teaspoon salt
- 1 teaspoon freshly ground black pepper
- ½ teaspoon cayenne pepper
- 1 cup (250 ml) water

Preheat the oven to 425°F (220°C/gas 7). Make small incisions in the lamb. Combine the butter, garlic, paprika, cumin, coriander, cinnamon, salt, black pepper, and cayenne pepper in a small bowl. Rub the spiced butter over the lamb, forcing it into the incisions.

Place the lamb in a large roasting pan and pour in the water. Bake on the top shelf for 20 minutes. Move the lamb to the middle shelf, reduce the heat to 300°F (150°C/gas 2), and bake for about 4 hours, until the meat is falling off the bone. Baste with the pan juices every 15 minutes to keep moist. Remove from the oven, cover with foil, and let rest for 15 minutes. Serve hot.

SERVES **6** • PREPARATION **15** MIN. • COOKING 4½ HR. • LEVEL **1**

14 braised beef in barolo

- 3 pounds (1.5 kg) boneless beef roast, preferably chuck
- 1 onion, sliced
- 1 carrot, sliced
- 1 stalk celery, sliced
- 2 bay leaves
- 1 teaspoon peppercorns
- 3 cups (750 ml bottle) Barolo wine (or another dry, robust red wine)
- 1/3 cup (90 ml) extra-virgin olive oil
- 1 tablespoon butter
- Salt
- Garlic mash (see page 285), to serve

Place the meat in a bowl with the onion, carrot, celery, bay leaves, and peppercorns. Cover with the wine and place in the refrigerator to marinate for 24 hours. Drain, reserving the marinade. Strain the marinade, reserving the wine. Tie the meat firmly with kitchen string.

Heat the oil and butter over medium heat in a heavy-bottomed saucepan just large enough to hold the meat. Add the meat, season with salt, and brown on all sides. Pour about half the wine over the meat, cover, and simmer until very tender, 3–4 hours. Add more wine during cooking, as required.

Slice the meat and place on a serving dish. Spoon the sauce over the top and serve hot with the garlic mash.

SERVES 6 • PREPARATION 15 MIN. + 24 HR. TO MARINATE • COOKING 3–4 HR. • LEVEL 1

15 roast leg of lamb
with aromatic herbs

- 3 slices sandwich bread
- 4 cloves garlic, chopped
- Mixture of aromatic herbs: 4 leaves sage, 1 twig rosemary, 1 twig thyme, 1 twig marjoram, 1 large bunch parsley
- Salt and freshly ground black pepper
- 2 tablespoons butter
- 1 leg of lamb, 3–4 pounds (1.5–2 kg), bone in
- ¼ cup (60 ml) extra-virgin olive oil
- 2 pounds (1 kg) potatoes, peeled
- ⅔ cup (150 ml) dry white wine

Cut the crusts off the bread and chop in a food processor with the garlic and aromatic herbs (leaves only). Season with salt and plenty of pepper.

Put the butter in a roasting pan and place in a preheated oven at 375°F (190°C/gas 5) for a few minutes, until the butter melts.

Place the lamb in the roasting pan, drizzle with the oil, and scatter with the chopped herbs and bread. Return to the oven and cook for 2 hours. Add the potatoes after about 1 hour. Baste the meat from time to time with the wine and cooking juices.

Transfer to a heated serving dish and serve hot.

SERVES 6 • PREPARATION 15 MIN. • COOKING 2 HR. • LEVEL 1

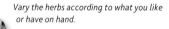

Vary the herbs according to what you like or have on hand.

16 chicken tagine
with pears & cinnamon

- ¹/₄ cup (60 g) butter
- 4 firm-ripe pears, peeled, cored, and quartered
- ¹/₄ teaspoon ground cardamom
- ¹/₄ cup (60 ml) honey
- ¹/₄ cup (60 ml) vegetable oil
- 2 onions, finely chopped
- 4 boneless skinless chicken breast halves
- ¹/₈ teaspoon saffron threads
- 2 teaspoons grated ginger
- Salt and freshly ground black pepper
- 1 cinnamon stick
- ¹/₃ cup (50 g) raisins
- Fresh cilantro (coriander)
- 2 tablespoon lemon juice
- 1 cup (250 ml) water
- 4 strips orange zest
- 3 orange slices, halved
- 2 fresh orange juice
- 2 tablespoons almonds

Melt the butter in a large saucepan over medium heat. Add the pears and sauté for 2 minutes. Sprinkle with the cardamom. Add the honey and gently turn the pears until lightly caramelized. Remove and set aside.

Add the oil to the pan and sauté the onions over low heat until golden, 10 minutes. Add the chicken, saffron, and ginger. Season with salt and pepper. Sauté over medium-high heat until seared all over, 2–3 minutes. Add the cinnamon stick, raisins, cilantro, lemon juice, and water. Bring to a boil, cover, and simmer until very tender, about 1 hour. Return the pears to the pan and add the orange zest, orange, and juice. Simmer for 15 minutes. Sprinkle with almonds and serve hot.

SERVES 4 • PREPARATION 15 MIN. • COOKING 1¹/₂ HR. • LEVEL 2

17 lamb tagine
with raisins, honey & almonds

- ¼ cup (60 ml) sunflower oil
- 3 tablespoons butter
- 2 teaspoons ground ginger
- Salt and white pepper
- ½ teaspoon ground turmeric
- 3 onions, 1 finely grated and 2 coarsely chopped
- 3 cloves garlic, finely chopped
- 2½ pounds (1.2 kg) lamb, cut into small chunks
- 1 tablespoon honey
- ¾ cup (120 g) raisins
- ½ cup (100 g) dried apricots
- Juice of 1 lemon
- 1 cinnamon stick
- ¼ cup (40 g) flaked almonds, toasted, to garnish
- Fresh cilantro (coriander)
- Freshly cooked couscous

Heat the oil and butter in the same pan over medium-high heat. Add the ginger, salt, pepper, turmeric, grated onion, and garlic. Sauté for 30 seconds.

Add the lamb, chopped onions, and honey. Pour in enough water to just cover the meat. Cover and simmer over low heat until the meat is almost tender, 2 hours. After the stew has been cooking for 1 hour, soak the raisins and apricots in a ladleful of the cooking liquid, the lemon juice, and a little hot water. Let soften for 30 minutes.

Add the fruit mixture and cinnamon. Cover and simmer until the lamb is completely tender. Sprinkle with almonds and cilantro. Serve hot with couscous.

SERVES 4 • PREPARATION 20 MIN. • COOKING 2 HR. • LEVEL 2

18 roasted veal roll
with potatoes

- 1 pound (500 g) slice of veal, preferably topside
- 1 black truffle, thinly sliced
- 2 tablespoons pistachios
- 2 tablespoons chopped pancetta
- 1 clove garlic, finely chopped
- Salt and freshly ground black pepper
- 2 sprigs rosemary
- 1/4 cup (60 g) butter
- 1/4 cup (60 g) extra-virgin olive oil
- 1/4 cup (60 ml) dry white wine
- 1 pound (500 g) potatoes, peeled and cut in bite-size pieces

Preheat the oven to 375°F (190°C/gas 5). Lay the veal slice out flat on a work surface. Use a sharp knife to trim the sides to make a fairly even rectangle. Pound lightly with a meat tenderizer, taking care not to break the meat.

Sprinkle with the truffle, pistachios, pancetta, garlic, and trimmings of veal. Season with salt and pepper.

Roll the veal up tightly, with the grain of the meat parallel to the length of the roll. Tie with kitchen string. Tuck the rosemary under the string against the roll. Place the roll in a roasting pan with the butter and oil and place in the oven. Turn often during roasting, basting with the wine and cooking juices.

After the meat has been cooking for about 1½ hours, add the potatoes, basting well in the cooking juices. Continue cooking until the potatoes are crisp and golden brown and the meat is very tender, about 45 minutes.

Serve hot with the potatoes.

SERVES 4 • PREPARATION 20 MIN. • COOKING 2¼ HR. • LEVEL 2

19 venison casserole

- 2 tablespoons extra-virgin olive oil
- $1^3/_4$ pounds (750 g) venison, cut into small chunks
- $^3/_4$ cup (90 g) diced pancetta
- 1 clove garlic, finely chopped
- 2 red onions, finely chopped
- 2 large carrots, finely chopped
- 2 firm-ripe tomatoes, coarsely chopped
- $^1/_2$ cup (120 ml) dry red wine
- 1 cup (250 ml) water + more as needed
- 1 sprig fresh rosemary
- 1 bay leaf
- 10 ounces (300 g) canned chestnuts
- Freshly cooked polenta, to serve (see page 214)

Preheat the oven to 300°F (150°C/gas 2). Heat the oil in a Dutch oven over medium-high heat. Add the venison and pancetta and sauté until browned, 5–8 minutes.

Add the garlic, onions, carrots, and tomatoes. Pour in the wine and water. Bring to a boil. Add the rosemary and bay leaf. Cover and bake for 1 hour.

Stir in the chestnuts. Bake, adding more water if the sauce starts to dry out, for 1 hour more, until the venison is very tender. Serve hot over the polenta.

SERVES 4–6 • PREPARATION 15 MIN. • COOKING $2^1/_4$ HR. • LEVEL 2

20 lamb & potato casserole

- 2 pounds (1 kg) lamb shoulder, boned, cut into bite-size pieces
- 2 pounds (1 kg) yellow, waxy potatoes, thickly sliced or cut into wedges
- 4 large tomatoes, quartered
- 1 onion, sliced
- 1/4 cup (60 ml) extra-virgin olive oil
- Salt and freshly ground black pepper
- Leaves from a small sprig of rosemary
- 1 teaspoon dried oregano
- 1 cup (250 ml) boiling water

Preheat the oven to 400°F (200°C/gas 6). Combine the lamb, potatoes, tomatoes, and onion in an ovenproof casserole. Drizzle with the oil and season with a little salt and plenty of pepper. Sprinkle with the rosemary and oregano.

Cover and bake until the meat is tender, about 2 hours. Baste at frequent intervals with a little boiling water. Serve hot.

SERVES **4–6** • PREPARATION **15** MIN. • COOKING **2** HR. • LEVEL **1**

thai chicken
salad

thai beef
salad

turkey & mango
curry

spicy beef burgers

spicy lamb burgers

TOP
20

lamb korma

spicy chicken fritters

spicy meatballs

bbq piri piri chicken

tex-mex chicken

bbq chicken
with spicy mexican salsa

12 beef curry with grapefruit

13 sichuan chicken

14 cajun chicken

spicy meat
dishes

15 peposo (tuscan black pepper stew)

16 chicken & pineapple stir-fry

17 chicken & walnut stir-fry

18 hot & spicy lamb stew

19 lamb curry

20 pork curry

1 thai chicken salad

- 2 stalks lemongrass, chopped
- 2 red chiles, seeded
- 3 cloves garlic
- 1 small piece fresh ginger
- 4 boneless skinless chicken breast halves
- 2 tablespoons sesame oil
- 1 teaspoon chile powder
- 3 tablespoons Thai fish sauce
- 1 red onion, chopped
- 3 tablespoons freshly squeezed lime juice
- 2 tablespoons each coarsely chopped fresh basil, mint, and cilantro (coriander)
- 2 small romaine (cos) lettuces, leaves separated
- 1 cucumber, diced
- 2 cups (100 g) bean sprouts
- Lime wedges, to serve

Blend the lemongrass, chiles, garlic, and ginger in a food processor until finely chopped. Set aside. Blend the chicken breasts in the processor until coarsely chopped.

Heat a wok over high heat with the sesame oil. Add the lemongrass mixture and stir-fry for 2 minutes. Add the chicken and chile powder and stir-fry for 4 minutes. Stir in the fish sauce. Simmer on medium for 4–5 minutes, stirring often. Add the onion and cook for 2 minutes.

Remove from the heat. Drizzle with the lime juice. Add the basil, mint, cilantro, lettuce, cucumber, and bean sprouts and toss well. Serve warm, garnished with lime.

SERVES 4–6 • PREPARATION 20 MIN. • COOKING 15 MIN. • LEVEL 1

2 thai beef salad

- 3 tablespoons freshly squeezed lime juice
- 2 tablespoons Thai fish sauce
- 1 tablespoon brown sugar
- 2 teaspoons Thai red curry paste
- 1 clove garlic, finely chopped
- 3 tablespoons peanut oil
- 1 pound (500 g) rump, fillet, or sirloin steak
- 3 cups (150 g) curly endive
- 1 cucumber, thinly sliced lengthwise
- 20 cherry tomatoes, halved
- 2 large red chiles, seeded and thinly sliced
- $1/3$ cup each fresh mint, cilantro (coriander), and basil
- $1^1/2$ cups (75 g) mung bean sprouts
- $1/4$ cup (40 g) roasted peanuts

Combine the lime juice, fish sauce, sugar, curry paste, garlic, and 1 tablespoon of oil in a medium bowl. Add the beef and toss to coat. Cover with plastic wrap (cling film) and marinate in the refrigerator for 2 hours.

Preheat a large frying pan on high heat with the remaining 2 tablespoons of oil. Drain the beef from the marinade and cook until browned, 2–3 minutes each side. Set aside for 5 minutes to rest.

Combine the endive, cucumber, tomatoes, chiles, mint, cilantro, and basil in a large bowl. Thinly slice the beef and add to the salad. Drizzle with the marinade, top with the bean sprouts and peanuts, and serve.

SERVES 4 • PREPARATION 20 MIN. + 2 HR. TO MARINATE • COOKING 4–6 MIN. • LEVEL 1

3 turkey & mango curry

Curry Paste
- 4 chiles, seeded and chopped
- 2 leeks, white part only, chopped
- 6 cloves garlic, chopped
- 1 bunch coriander root, chopped
- Zest of 2 limes, green part only
- 2 teaspoons cumin seeds
- 2 teaspoons Thai fish sauce

Curry
- 2 tablespoons peanut oil
- 1½ pounds (750 g) turkey breast, cut in bite-size chunks
- ¾ cup (180 ml) coconut milk
- 2 teaspoons sugar
- 3 teaspoons soy sauce
- 2 teaspoons Worcestershire sauce
- 2 small mangos, pitted and chopped
- Freshly cooked jasmine rice, to serve
- Fresh cilantro (coriander) leaves, to garnish

Curry Paste Blend the chiles, leeks, garlic, coriander root, lime zest, cumin, and fish sauce in a food processor until smooth.

Curry Heat the oil in a deep frying-pan over medium-high heat and add 1½ tablespoons of the curry paste. Cook for 2 minutes.

Add the turkey, coconut milk, sugar, soy sauce, and Worcestershire sauce. Stir well and bring to a boil. Reduce the heat and simmer until the turkey is tender, about 45 minutes.

Add the mangos and cook for 2 more minutes. Serve hot with the rice, garnished with cilantro.

SERVES 4–6 • PREPARATION 15 MIN. • COOKING 50 MIN. • LEVEL 1

You can replace the turkey in this recipe with chicken, if preferred. Add more or less chiles according to how hot and spicy you want the dish to be.

4 spicy beef burgers

- 4 tablespoons (60 ml) extra-virgin olive oil
- 2 small red onions, 1 grated and 1 thinly sliced
- 2 cloves garlic, minced
- 2 small red chiles, seeded and finely chopped
- 1 tablespoon hot paprika
- 2 teaspoons ground cumin
- 1 teaspoon ground turmeric
- Salt and freshly ground black pepper
- 1¼ pounds (600 g) ground (minced) beef
- ⅓ cup (50 g) fine dry bread crumbs
- 3 tablespoons finely chopped fresh parsley
- 1 large egg, lightly beaten
- 4 slices Cheddar cheese
- 4 burger buns, halved and toasted
- Lettuce, shredded
- 2 tomatoes, sliced
- Barbecue sauce

Heat 2 tablespoons of oil in a frying pan over medium heat. Add the grated onion, garlic, and chiles and sauté until softened, 3–4 minutes. Stir in the paprika, cumin, turmeric, salt, and pepper. Set aside to cool. Blend the beef, bread crumbs, parsley, egg, and onion mixture in a food processor. Shape into four burgers.

Preheat a frying pan over high heat. Drizzle with the remaining 2 tablespoons of oil and cook the burgers until browned, 2–3 minutes each side. Put a slice of cheese on each burger and let melt slightly.

Cover the bases of the buns with lettuce, tomato, and sliced onion. Put the burgers on top, spread with barbecue sauce, and cover with the lids. Serve hot.

SERVES 4 • PREPARATION 15 MIN. • COOKING 8–10 MINUTES • LEVEL 1

5 spicy lamb burgers

- 2 small red onions,
  1 chopped, 1 sliced
- 2 cloves garlic, minced
- 2 large red chiles, seeded
  and coarsely chopped
- 2 tablespoons fresh cilantro
  (coriander)
- 1¼ pounds (600 g) ground
  (minced) lamb
- ½ cup (75 g) dry bread crumbs
- 1 large egg, lightly beaten
- 1 teaspoon ground cumin
- 1 teaspoon ground coriander
- 1 teaspoon salt
- ½ teaspoon ground
  cinnamon
- ¼ teaspoon freshly ground
  black pepper
- 2 tablespoons extra-virgin
  olive oil
- 4 burger buns, halved
- 1½ cups (75 g) curly endive
- ½ cup (120 ml) ketchup
- 2 tomatoes, diced

Combine the chopped onion, garlic, chiles, and cilantro in a food processor. Blend to make a coarse paste. Add the lamb, bread crumbs, egg, cumin, coriander, salt, cinnamon, and pepper and blend to just combine. Transfer the mixture to a bowl and shape into four even-size burgers. Cover and refrigerate for 1 hour.

Preheat a grill pan or barbecue on medium-high heat. Drizzle with the oil and grill the burgers, 3–4 minutes on each side. Lightly grill the buns.

Cover the bases of the buns with endive and sliced onion. Top with the burgers, a dollop of ketchup, and the tomatoes. Cover with the lids and serve warm.

SERVES 4 • PREPARATION 15 MIN. + 1 HR. TO CHILL • COOKING 6–8 MIN. • LEVEL 1

6 lamb korma

Spice Mix
- 10 cloves
- 10 black peppercorns
- 4 cardamom pods
- 1 cinnamon stick
- 4 dried red chiles
- 4 tablespoons coriander seeds
- 2 tablespoons cumin seeds
- 1 teaspoon fennel seeds
- 1 star anise
- 1 teaspoon turmeric powder

Korma
- 2 tablespoons vegetable oil
- 1¼ pounds (600 g) lamb leg, cut into cubes
- 2 onions, thinly sliced
- ½ tablespoon finely grated ginger
- 1 clove garlic, finely chopped
- 1 teaspoon chile powder
- Salt
- ½ teaspoon saffron strands, soaked in ¼ cup (60 ml) warm water
- 4 ounces (120 g) cashews, blended to a paste with 2 tablespoons water
- 1 cinnamon stick
- 1 cup (250 ml) plain yogurt
- 2 tomatoes, chopped
- Freshly cooked basmati rice
- Fresh cilantro (coriander)

Spice Mix Toast all the spices, except the turmeric, in a dry frying pan until fragrant, about 30 seconds. Let cool slightly. Grind the toasted spices and turmeric to a powder with a pestle and mortar or spice grinder.

Korma Heat 1 tablespoon of oil in a wok over medium-high heat. Add the lamb and stir-fry until browned all over, 5–8 minutes. Remove the lamb and set aside.

Heat the remaining 1 tablespoon of oil in the wok and sauté the onions, ginger, garlic, spice mix, and chile powder until fragrant, 1–2 minutes.

Return the lamb to the wok, season with salt, and stir until well combined. Stir in the saffron and soaking water, cashew paste, and cinnamon stick, then pour in enough water to just cover the lamb. Bring to a boil, then cover and simmer over low heat, stirring occasionally, until the meat is very tender, about 1½ hours. Add more water if the mixture begins to dry out.

Stir in the yogurt and tomatoes and simmer for 1–2 minutes. Serve hot with the rice, garnished with the cilantro.

SERVES 4 • PREPARATION 30 MIN. • COOKING 2 HR. • LEVEL 2

7 spicy chicken fritters

- 2 slices white sandwich bread, crusts removed
- $^1/_4$ cup (60 ml) milk
- $1^1/_4$ pounds (600 g) ground (minced) chicken
- 1 large egg, lightly beaten
- Salt and freshly ground black pepper
- 1–2 teaspoons hot paprika
- $^1/_2$ cup (75 g) all-purpose (plain) flour
- 1 cup (250 ml) vegetable oil for frying
- Freshly squeezed juice of $^1/_2$ lemon

Soak the bread in the milk in a small bowl for 5 minutes. Drain well, squeezing out excess milk. Mix the chicken, soaked bread, and egg in a large bowl. Season with salt, pepper, and paprika. Use your hands to shape into small round fritters. Roll in the flour.

Heat the oil to very hot in a large deep frying pan. Fry the fritters in batches until golden brown, about 5 minutes each batch. Drain on paper towels. Drizzle with the lemon juice and serve hot.

SERVES 4 • PREPARATION 20 MIN. • COOKING 10–15 MIN. • LEVEL 1

8 spicy meatballs

- 5 tablespoons vegetable oil
- 1 large onion, finely chopped
- 2 cloves garlic, thinly sliced
- 14 ounces (400 g) ground (minced) beef
- 8 ounces (250 g) ground (minced) pork
- 2 chiles, finely chopped
- $1/2$ teaspoon salt
- $1/4$ teaspoon coarsely ground black pepper
- $1/2$ teaspoon Dijon mustard
- 1 teaspoon hot paprika
- $3/4$ inch (2 cm) fresh ginger, peeled and grated
- 2 tablespoons fine dry bread crumbs
- 2 tablespoons finely chopped fresh parsley
- 1 large egg, beaten

Heat 2 tablespoons of oil in a large frying pan over medium heat. Add the onion and garlic and sauté until softened, 3–4 minutes.

Mix the beef and pork in a bowl. Add the onion mixture. Stir in the chiles, salt, pepper, mustard, paprika, ginger, bread crumbs, parsley, and egg and mix well using your hands. Shape into about 20 small meatballs.

Heat the remaining 3 tablespoons of oil in a large frying pan over medium-high heat. Fry the meatballs until golden and cooked through, 5–10 minutes. Serve hot.

SERVES 4–6 • PREPARATION 15 MIN. • COOKING 10–15 MIN. • LEVEL 1

9 bbq piri piri chicken

Marinade
- ½ cup (120 ml) extra-virgin olive oil
- ⅓ cup (90 ml) freshly squeezed lemon juice
- 6 small red chiles
- 3 cloves garlic, coarsely chopped
- 1 tablespoon coarsely chopped fresh ginger
- 1 teaspoon sweet paprika
- 1 teaspoon salt
- 4 tablespoons finely chopped fresh parsley

Chicken
- 1 chicken, weighing about 4 pounds (2 kg)
- Mixed salad greens, to serve
- Lemon wedges, to serve

Marinade Combine the oil, lemon juice, chiles, garlic, ginger, paprika, and salt in a small saucepan over medium heat and bring to a boil. Simmer for 2 minutes. Let cool, then pour into a food processor and blend until smooth. Transfer to a large bowl with the parsley.

Chicken Put the chicken breast-side down on a clean chopping board. Remove the backbone using a sharp knife or kitchen scissors. Wash under cold running water. Splay the chicken out flat. Insert two metal skewers through the chicken beginning at the thickest part of the breast all the way through to the thighs. This will ensure the chicken stays splayed. Score the chicken in the thickest part of the legs, to help it to cook more evenly. Coat the chicken in the marinade, cover, and refrigerate for at least 4 hours or overnight.

Preheat a barbecue grill on medium heat. Cook the chicken until the juices run clear from the thickest part of the thigh, 15–20 minutes. Baste with marinade during cooking to keep it moist. Remove the skewers and serve hot with the salad and lemon wedges.

SERVES 4 • PREPARATION 20 MIN. + 4–12 HR. TO MARINATE • COOKING 15–20 MIN. • LEVEL 2

Piri piri chicken is a Portuguese dish that comes originally from Mozambique (an ex-colony of Portugal) where piri piri chiles are grown. You can use any small, fiery red chile.

10 tex-mex chicken

Marinade
- 8 small red chiles, seeded and chopped
- 2 tablespoons chile paste
- 1 cup (250 ml) extra-virgin olive oil
- 15 large cloves garlic, peeled and coarsely chopped
- 1 heaped teaspoon salt
- Freshly squeezed juice of 2–3 limes
- 3 tablespoons finely chopped fresh cilantro (coriander)

Chicken
- 10 chicken drumsticks

Marinade Blend the chiles and chile paste in a food processor until smooth. Warm the oil in a medium saucepan over low heat. Add the garlic and blended chile paste and simmer over very low heat until the garlic is soft but not browned, 35–40 minutes. Let cool. Stir in the salt, lime juice, and cilantro.

Chicken Put the marinade in a glass or stainless steel bowl. Add the chicken and marinate for 6–8 hours.

Preheat a grill pan or barbecue on high heat. Drain the chicken and grill until the chicken is tender, 15–20 minutes. Serve hot.

SERVES 4 • PREPARATION 15 MIN. + 6–8 HR. TO MARINATE
COOKING 15–20 MIN. • LEVEL 1

11 bbq chicken
with spicy mexican salsa

Chicken
- 8 chicken drumsticks
- 2 tablespoons sesame oil
- 1 clove garlic, finely chopped
- 1 tablespoon sweet paprika
- 2 teaspoons ground cumin
- 1 teaspoon chile powder
- Salt and freshly ground black pepper
- Sour cream to serve

Salsa
- 2 cups (300 g) corn (sweetcorn)
- 2 teaspoons sesame oil
- 1 large tomato, diced
- 1 avocado, pitted and diced
- 1/2 small red onion, diced
- 1/2 cup (25 g) fresh cilantro (coriander) leaves
- 1 red chile, finely chopped
- 2 tablespoons freshly squeezed lime juice

Chicken Score the drumsticks with a sharp knife. Combine the oil, garlic, paprika, cumin, and chile powder in a bowl. Add the chicken and turn to coat. Season with salt and pepper. Cover and marinate overnight in the refrigerator.

Salsa Combine the corn, oil, tomato, avocado, onion, cilantro, chile, lime juice, salt, and pepper in a bowl.

Preheat a grill pan or barbecue on high heat. Grill the drumsticks until browned and cooked through, 10–15 minutes. Serve hot with the salsa and sour cream.

SERVES 4 • PREPARATION 20 MIN. + 12 HR. TO MARINATE • COOKING 10–15 MIN. • LEVEL 1

12 beef curry
with grapefruit

Garam Masala
- 2 teaspoons cardamom seeds
- 1 teaspoon cloves
- 1 cinnamon stick, broken into pieces
- 2 tablespoons cumin seeds
- 2 tablespoons coriander seeds
- 1 tablespoon black peppercorns

Beef Curry
- $1/4$ cup (60 ml) vegetable oil
- 10 cloves
- 10 green cardamom pods, lightly crushed
- 2 onions, thinly sliced
- 8 cloves garlic, crushed
- 1 tablespoon finely grated ginger
- 1 teaspoon turmeric powder
- 3 teaspoons chile powder
- 4 teaspoons ground cumin
- 4 teaspoons ground coriander
- 2 teaspoons salt
- 3 pounds (1.5 kg) chuck steak, cut in small cubes
- 3 tablespoons ketchup
- $3 1/2$ ounces (100 g) ghee
- $2 1/4$ cups (300 ml) water
- Finely grated zest, juice, and flesh of 1 grapefruit
- $1/2$ teaspoon freshly ground black pepper

Garam Masala Heat a heavy-based frying pan over very low heat. Add all the garam masala ingredients to the pan and toast until aromatic. This will take 2–3 minutes. Shake the pan and take care not to let the spices burn. Transfer to a spice grinder and grind to a fine powder. Measure out 2 teaspoons for the curry. Store the rest in a screwtop jar for future use.

Beef Curry Heat the oil in a large, heavy-bottomed pan over medium heat. Add the cloves and cardamom pods and let sizzle for a few seconds. Add the onions and simmer over low heat, stirring occasionally, until very soft and pale brown, 20–30 minutes.

Stir in the garlic, ginger, turmeric, chile powder, cumin, coriander, and salt. Simmer for one minute, then add the beef and cook, stirring frequently, for 10 minutes. Add the ketchup and ghee and simmer 2–3 minutes. Add the water, cover, and simmer until the beef is almost tender, about $1 1/2$ hours.

After the curry has been cooking for $1 1/2$ hours, add the grapefruit zest and juice and the garam masala and simmer, uncovered, until the beef is very tender, about 30 minutes. Season with salt and pepper. Garnish with pieces of grapefruit flesh and serve hot.

SERVES 6–8 • PREPARATION 30 MIN. • COOKING $2 3/4$ HR. • LEVEL 2

13 sichuan chicken

- 1¾ pounds (800 g) chicken thigh fillets, halved
- 3 tablespoons vegetable oil
- 1 clove garlic, finely chopped
- 2 teaspoons finely grated fresh ginger
- 1 teaspoon Sichuan peppercorns, finely crushed
- 1 teaspoon chile paste
- ½ cup (120 ml) chicken stock
- 3 tablespoons soy sauce
- 1 tablespoon Chinese rice vinegar
- ½ tablespoon sugar
- ½ teaspoon dried red pepper flakes
- Freshly cooked basmati rice, to serve
- Steamed Chinese broccoli, to serve

Preheat a large wok over high heat. Coat the chicken in 2 tablespoons of oil and sauté until browned, 4–5 minutes. Set aside.

Decrease the heat to medium-low and add the remaining 1 tablespoon of oil. Stir-fry the garlic and ginger until softened, about 2 minutes. Add the peppercorns and chile paste and stir-fry until fragrant, about 30 seconds. Return the chicken to the wok. Add the stock, soy sauce, rice vinegar, sugar, and red pepper flakes. Simmer, stirring occasionally, until cooked, 10–15 minutes. Serve hot with the rice and broccoli.

SERVES 4–6 • PREPARATION 15 MIN. • COOKING 20–25 MIN. • LEVEL 1

14 cajun chicken

- 2 tablespoons vegetable oil
- 1 tablespoon freshly squeezed lemon juice
- 1 tablespoon dried oregano
- 1 tablespoon dried thyme
- 1 tablespoon sweet paprika
- 1 tablespoon garlic powder
- 1 teaspoon cayenne pepper
- 1 teaspoon freshly ground black pepper
- 1/2 teaspoon ground cumin
- 1/2 teaspoon salt
- 4 boneless skinless chicken breast halves
- 2 lemons, halved
- Mixed salad greens, to serve

Combine the oil, lemon juice, oregano, thyme, paprika, garlic powder, cayenne, black pepper, cumin, and salt in a small bowl.

Preheat a large frying pan over medium-high heat. Coat the chicken breasts in the spice mix. Cook until blackened and cooked through, 5–10 minutes.

Preheat a small frying pan over medium-high heat. Cook the lemons, flesh side down until blackened, 1–2 minutes. Serve hot with the salad and lemons.

SERVES 4 • PREPARATION 10 MIN. • COOKING 5–10 MIN. • LEVEL 1

15 peposo
(tuscan black pepper stew)

- 3½ pounds (1.7 kg) muscle from veal shanks, cut in bite-sized pieces
- 4 cloves garlic, finely chopped
- 1½ pounds (750 g) tomatoes, peeled and chopped
- Salt
- 4 tablespoons freshly ground black pepper
- 4 cups (1 liter) cold water
- 1½ cups (350 ml) robust, dry red wine
- Boiled or steamed potatoes and other mixed vegetables, to serve

Place the meat in a large, heavy-bottomed saucepan with the garlic, tomatoes, salt, and black pepper. Pour in just enough of the water to cover the meat.

Simmer over low heat for 2 hours, adding extra water as the sauce becomes too dry. Stir from time to time. After 2 hours, pour in the wine and cook for 1 hour more, until the meat is very tender.

Serve hot with the potatoes and other vegetables.

SERVES 8 • PREPARATION 15 MIN. • COOKING 3 HR. • LEVEL 1

This is an unusual dish in Tuscan cuisine, but it is an old and widely served classic. Don't be afraid to add 4 tablespoons of freshly ground black pepper. The stew simmers for several hours and the pepper gains depth to balance its bite.

16 chicken & pineapple stir-fry

- 12 ounces (350 g) Chinese egg noodles
- 4 tablespoons (60 ml) vegetable oil
- 4 boneless skinless chicken breast halves, cut into thin strips
- 1 tablespoon finely minced fresh ginger
- 2 cloves garlic, finely chopped
- 2 cups (300 g) cubed fresh pineapple
- 3 tablespoons molasses (treacle)
- 4 cups (200 g) baby spinach
- 8 shiitake mushrooms, caps quartered and stems diced
- 2 tablespoons freshly squeezed lemon juice
- 1 teaspoon Tabasco
- ½ teaspoon red pepper flakes
- 4 tablespoons toasted sesame seeds

Cook the noodles according to the instructions on the package. Heat 2 tablespoons of oil in a wok over medium-high heat. Add the chicken, ginger, and garlic and stir-fry until the chicken is white, 6–8 minutes. Set aside. Add the pineapple and molasses to the same pan. Stir-fry until the pineapple is brown and tender, about 2 minutes. Set aside with the chicken.

Heat the remaining oil in the wok and add the spinach, noodles, mushrooms, lemon juice, Tabasco, and red pepper flakes. Stir-fry until the just tender, about 5 minutes. Return the chicken and pineapple to the wok and stir-fry over high heat until hot, about 2 minutes. Sprinkle with the sesame seeds and serve.

SERVES 4 • PREPARATION 15 MIN. • COOKING 15 MIN. • LEVEL 1

17 chicken & walnut stir-fry

- 2 tablespoons peanut oil
- 1 cup (150 g) coarsely chopped walnuts
- 4 boneless skinless chicken breast halves, cut into chunks
- 4 cloves garlic, thinly sliced
- 1 teaspoon red chile paste
- 8 ounces (250 g) green beans, cut into short lengths
- 4 ounces (120 g) water chestnuts, finely chopped
- 1 green bell pepper (capsicum), thinly sliced
- 1 cup (250 ml) chicken stock
- 2 tablespoons lime juice
- 1 tablespoon light soy sauce
- 2 tablespoons peanut butter
- 2 tablespoons boiling water
- Freshly cooked noodles

Heat the oil in a large wok over medium-high heat. Stir-fry the walnuts until toasted, about 5 minutes. Remove with a slotted spoon and set aside on paper towels.

Add the chicken and garlic to the wok and stir-fry until the chicken is lightly browned, 6–8 minutes. Add the chile paste, green beans, water chestnuts, and bell pepper. Stir-fry for 5 minutes. Add the chicken stock, lime juice, and soy sauce. Mix over medium-low heat until the ingredients are blended.

Stir in the peanut butter and water and sprinkle with the walnuts. Serve hot with the noodles.

SERVES 4–6 • PREPARATION 15 MIN. • COOKING 15–20 MIN. • LEVEL 1

18 hot & spicy lamb stew

- ¼ cup (60 ml) extra-virgin olive oil
- 1 onion, finely chopped
- 1 carrot, finely chopped
- 1 stalk celery, finely chopped
- 2 cloves garlic, finely chopped
- 2 tablespoons finely chopped parsley
- 2 dried chiles, crumbled or 1 teaspoon red pepper flakes
- ½ cup (60 g) diced pancetta
- 2¼ pounds (1.2 kg) lamb, shoulder or leg, cut in pieces
- Salt and freshly ground black pepper
- ⅔ cup (150 ml) dry white wine
- 1 pound (500 g) peeled and chopped ripe tomatoes
- Freshly cooked rice, to serve

Heat the oil over medium-high heat in a large, heavy-bottomed pan, preferably earthenware. Add the onion, carrot, celery, garlic, parsley, chiles, and pancetta and sauté until golden brown, 5–8 minutes.

Add the lamb and sauté with the vegetable mixture, for 7–8 minutes more. Season with salt and pepper and pour in the wine. Cook until the wine has evaporated.

Add the tomatoes, lower the heat to low and partially cover. Cook until the meat is very tender, about 2 hours, adding a little hot water if the sauce reduces too much. Serve hot with boiled rice.

SERVES 4–6 • PREPARATION 15 MIN. • COOKING 2¼ HR. • LEVEL 1

The longer you leave this tasty stew to cook the more tender the lamb becomes. Add more or less chiles according to how spicy you like your food. Delicious with rice, the stew is also very good with mashed potatoes or freshly made polenta.

19 lamb curry

Spice Mix
- 1 teaspoon garam masala
- 1 teaspoon ground cumin
- 1 teaspoon ground coriander
- 1 teaspoon ground turmeric
- $1/2$ teaspoon ground cayenne

Curry
- 4 tablespoons (60 ml) vegetable oil
- 4 large lamb shanks
- 2 onions, thickly sliced
- 2 cloves garlic, finely chopped
- 2 teaspoons grated ginger
- 2 cardamom pods, split
- 2 bay leaves
- 1 cinnamon stick
- 2 cups (500 ml) chicken stock
- 1 (14-ounce/400-g) can tomatoes, with juice
- $1/3$ cup (90 g) plain yogurt
- 3 tablespoons finely chopped fresh cilantro (coriander)
- Freshly cooked basmati rice

Spice Mix Combine the garam masala, cumin, coriander, turmeric, and cayenne pepper in a small bowl.

Curry Preheat 2 tablespoons of oil in a large pan over high heat. Sauté the lamb until browned, 2–3 minutes each side. Set aside. Heat the remaining oil in the same pan over medium heat. Add the onions, garlic, and ginger and sauté until softened, 3–4 minutes. Add the spice mix, cardamom, bay leaves, and cinnamon and sauté until fragrant, about 1 minute. Add the chicken stock, tomatoes, and lamb and bring to a boil. Simmer until the lamb is falling off the bone, about 2 hours. Stir in the yogurt and cilantro. Serve hot with the rice.

SERVES 4 • PREPARATION 15 MIN. • COOKING 2 HR. • LEVEL 1

20 pork curry

Curry Paste
- 8 dried red chiles, crumbled
- 1 tablespoon coriander seeds
- 2 teaspoons cumin seeds
- 2 teaspoons peppercorns
- 1 teaspoon cardamom seeds
- 1 teaspoon ground cinnamon
- 5 cloves
- 2 tablespoons water
- 4 cloves garlic, chopped
- 1 teaspoon grated ginger
- $^1/_2$ teaspoon salt

Curry
- $1^1/_4$ pounds (600 g) pork fillet, diced
- 2 onions, thinly sliced
- 2 tablespoons white vinegar
- 2 bay leaves
- 3 tablespoons vegetable oil
- $^1/_2$ cup (120 ml) water

Curry Paste Dry-fry the chiles, coriander, cumin, peppercorns, cardamom, cinnamon, and cloves in a small frying pan over medium heat until fragrant, 1–2 minutes. Pound to make a fine powder. Add the water, garlic, ginger, and salt to make a paste.

Curry Combine the pork, onions, vinegar, and bay leaves in a medium bowl. Add the spice paste and toss to coat. Cover and refrigerate for 2 hours to marinate.

Heat the oil in a large pan over high heat. Drain the pork and sauté until browned, 3–4 minutes. Add the marinade and water and bring to a boil. Simmer over low heat until very tender, about 2 hours. Serve hot.

SERVES 4 • PREPARATION 15 MIN. + 2 HR. TO MARINATE • COOKING 2 HR. • LEVEL 1

lamb salad
with tzatziki

steak salad

meat & veggie skewers

sausage risotto with red wine

chicken risotto with white wine

TOP
20

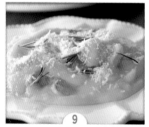

chicken fried rice

lamb stir-fry
with bell peppers

chicken stir-fry
with cashews & mango

pork & veggies
with polenta

beef & spinach stir-fry

spicy beef noodle stir-fry

turkey breast in pancetta
with veggies

pork & chorizo paella

arroz con pollo
(spanish rice with chicken)

one-dish
meals

chicken balls with veggies

lamb pilau

chicken biryani

roast pork shanks
with mixed vegetables

corned beef
with vegetables

fillet steak
with spicy vegetables

1 lamb salad
with tzatziki

Lamb Salad
- 3 tablespoons extra-virgin olive oil
- 1 pound (500 g) lamb steak, cut from the fillet
- 16 cherry tomatoes, halved
- 4 cups (200 g) arugula (rocket)
- Salt and freshly ground black pepper

Tzatziki
- 1 cup (250 ml) plain Greek-style yogurt
- 2 cloves garlic, finely chopped
- 1 small cucumber, peeled and cut into small dice
- 1 tablespoon finely chopped fresh mint
- 1 tablespoon extra-virgin olive oil
- 1 tablespoon freshly squeezed lemon juice

Lamb Salad Preheat a grill pan or barbecue on high heat. Brush the lamb with the oil. Place on the grill and cook until tender, 3–5 minutes each side for medium-rare. Put the tomatoes and arugula on a serving dish. Slice the lamb and place over the salad. Season with salt and pepper.

Tzatziki Whisk the yogurt, garlic, cucumber, mint, oil, and lemon juice in a bowl. Serve the lamb salad warm with tzatziki spooned over the top.

SERVES 4 • PREPARATION 10 MIN. • COOKING 6–10 MIN. • LEVEL 1

2 steak salad

- 2 pounds (1 kg) tenderloin steak
- Salt and freshly ground black pepper
- 6 tablespoons (90 ml) extra-virgin olive oil
- 4 cups (200 g) arugula (rocket)
- 20 cherry tomatoes, halved
- $1/4$ cup (60 ml) balsamic vinegar

Season the steak generously with salt and pepper. Preheat a grill pan or barbecue on high heat. Add 2 tablespoons of oil and cook the steaks for 8–15 minutes, depending on how you like your steak.

Arrange the arugula and tomatoes on serving plates. Slice the steak and place on top of the salads. Drizzle with the remaining 4 tablespoons of oil and the balsamic vinegar. Season with salt and pepper and serve hot.

SERVES 4–6 • PREPARATION 10 MIN. • COOKING 8–15 MIN. • LEVEL 1

3   meat & veggie skewers

- 12 ounces (350 g) pork
- 12 ounces (350 g) boned veal shoulder or shank
- 2 boneless skinless chicken breast halves
- 1 red bell pepper (capsicum)
- 1 yellow bell pepper (capsicum)
- 12 ounces (350 g) baby onions
- 20 cherry tomatoes
- 5 thick slices crusty bread
- 3 fresh Italian pork sausages
- 20 leaves fresh sage
- Salt and freshly ground black pepper
- $1/4$ cup (60 ml) extra-virgin olive oil
- $1/2$ cup (120 ml) beef stock

Preheat the oven to 400°F (200°C/gas 6). Remove any fat from the meat. Chop the meat, vegetables, and bread into large cubes or squares. Slice the sausages thickly.

Thread the cubes of meat and vegetables onto steel or wooden skewers, alternating pieces of meat, sausage, vegetables, bread, and sage leaves.

Arrange the skewers in a roasting dish and season with salt and pepper. Drizzle with the oil.

Bake for 30 minutes, turning occasionally and adding beef stock to moisten as required. When the meat is well browned, remove from the oven and serve hot.

SERVES 6 • PREPARATION 20 MIN. • COOKING 30 MIN. • LEVEL 1

Vary the meat and vegetables according to what you like or what you have on hand. Be sure to use choice cuts of beef or lamb that will cook quickly without becoming tough and chewy.

4 sausage risotto
with red wine

- 3 tablespoons extra-virgin olive oil
- 12 leaves fresh sage
- 2 tablespoons butter
- 1 large onion, finely chopped
- 14 ounces (400 g) Italian pork sausages, skinned and cut into bite-size pieces
- 2 cups (400 g) Italian risotto rice (Arborio, Carnaroli)
- 1/3 cup (90 ml) dry red wine
- 6 cups (1.5 liters) vegetable stock, boiling

Heat the oil in a small frying pan over medium heat. Add the sage and fry until crisp, about 2 minutes. Scoop out with a slotted spoon and drain on paper towels.

Melt the butter in a large frying pan over medium heat. Add the onion and sauté until softened, 3–4 minutes. Add the sausages and sauté until browned, about 5 minutes. Add the rice and sauté until translucent, about 2 minutes. Stir in the wine and cook until it evaporates, 2–3 minutes. Begin adding the stock, 1/2 cup (120 ml) at a time, cooking and stirring until each addition has been absorbed and the rice is tender, 15–18 minutes. Remove from the heat. Cover and let rest for 2–3 minutes. Garnish with the sage leaves and serve hot.

SERVES 4–6 • PREPARATION 20 MIN. • COOKING 30–35 MIN. • LEVEL 2

5 chicken risotto
with white wine

- ¼ cup (60 ml) extra-virgin olive oil
- 4 tablespoons (60 g) butter
- 1 onion, finely chopped
- 1 carrot, finely chopped
- 1 stalk celery, finely chopped
- 1 chicken, weighing about 3 pounds (1.5 kg), cut into 6 pieces
- 8 cups (2 liters) chicken stock, boiling
- 2 cups (400 g) Italian risotto rice (Arborio, Carnaroli)
- ½ cup (120 ml) dry white wine
- Salt and freshly ground black pepper
- ½ cup (60 g) freshly grated Parmesan cheese

Heat the oil and 2 tablespoons of butter in a large, frying pan over medium heat. Add the onion, carrot, and celery and sauté until softened, 5–7 minutes. Add the chicken and brown, 6–8 minutes. Add ½ cup (120 ml) of the stock, partly cover the pan, and simmer until the chicken is almost tender, about 30 minutes.

Add the rice and stir well. Pour in the wine and cook until evaporated, 2–3 minutes. Begin adding stock, ½ cup (120 ml) at a time. Cook and stir until each addition is absorbed and the rice is tender, 15–18 minutes. Stir in the remaining 2 tablespoons of butter. Season with salt and pepper. Sprinkle with the Parmesan and serve hot.

SERVES 4–6 • PREPARATION 20 MIN. • COOKING 1 HR. • LEVEL 2

6 chicken fried rice

- 3 tablespoons peanut oil
- 2 large eggs, lightly beaten
- 1 onion, finely chopped
- 2 cloves garlic, finely chopped
- 4 ounces (120 g) bacon slices, chopped
- 3 tablespoons Shaoxing wine or dry sherry
- 2 teaspoons sugar
- 4 cups (400 g) cooked shredded chicken
- 1/2 cup (75 g) frozen green peas
- 4 cups (400 g) cooked basmati or jasmine rice
- 3 tablespoons soy sauce
- 1 tablespoon Chinese oyster sauce
- 4 scallions (spring onions), thinly sliced diagonally

Heat a wok over high heat until hot. Add 1 tablespoon of oil. Pour in the eggs and cook, stirring constantly, until set, about 2 minutes. Transfer to a cutting board and cut into long strips.

Heat the remaining oil in a wok over high heat. Add the onion, garlic, and bacon. Stir-fry until tender, 2–3 minutes. Add the wine and sugar. Stir-fry for 1 minute. Add the chicken and peas. Stir-fry for 1 minute.

Add the rice, soy sauce, oyster sauce, scallions, and half the eggs to the wok. Stir-fry until the rice is hot, 2–3 minutes. Spoon into serving bowls. Sprinkle with the remaining egg and serve hot.

SERVES 4–6 • PREPARATION 15 MIN. • COOKING 10 MIN. • LEVEL 1

This is a delicious way to use up leftover rice. You can vary the recipe by using cooked leftover fish or steak instead of the chicken. Alternatively, you could buy 14 ounces (400 g) of cooked, peeled shrimp (prawns).

7 lamb stir-fry
with bell peppers

- ¹/₄ cup (60 ml) peanut oil
- 1¹/₂ pounds (750 g) lamb sirloin, cut into thin strips
- ¹/₄ teaspoon ground turmeric
- 1 teaspoon chile powder
- ¹/₂ teaspoon finely chopped fresh ginger
- 2 cloves garlic, finely chopped
- 1 teaspoon garam masala
- Salt
- 3 bell peppers (capsicums), mixed colors, thinly sliced
- 2 carrots, cut into thin sticks
- 4 canned water chestnuts, cut into eighths
- 2 tablespoons light soy sauce
- 2 tablespoons oyster sauce
- Freshly cooked basmati rice
- Green chiles, sliced

Heat the oil in a large wok over high heat. Add the lamb and sauté until lightly browned, about 8 minutes. Add the turmeric, chile powder, ginger, garlic, garam masala, and salt. Stir-fry to combine the flavors and finish cooking the lamb, about 5 minutes. Remove the lamb with a slotted spoon and set aside.

Add the bell peppers, carrots, and water chestnuts to the wok over medium-high heat, and stir-fry until the vegetables are crisp but tender, about 5 minutes. Return the lamb to the wok and add the soy and oyster sauces. Stir-fry until the dish begins to bubble. Serve hot with the rice and chiles.

SERVES 4 • PREPARATION 15 MIN. • COOKING 20 MIN. • LEVEL 1

8 chicken stir-fry
with cashews & mango

- 3 tablespoons peanut oil
- 1 onion, thinly sliced
- 2 bell peppers (capsicum), mixed colors, thinly sliced
- 3 carrots, julienned
- 1 (4-ounce/120-g) can bamboo shoots, drained
- 2 boneless skinless chicken breasts, cut into small cubes
- 1 mango, peeled and cut into small pieces
- 2 tablespoons freshly squeezed lime juice
- 1 tablespoon cornstarch (cornflour)
- 1 tablespoon dark soy sauce
- Fresh cilantro (coriander)
- 1 cup (100 g) roasted cashews
- Freshly cooked basmati rice

Heat the oil in a large wok over high heat. Add the onion, bell peppers, carrots, and bamboo shoots. Stir-fry until the vegetables are crisp but tender, about 5 minutes. Add the chicken and stir-fry until it turns white, about 5 minutes. Add the mango and stir-fry gently for 2 minutes.

Mix the lime juice, cornstarch, and soy sauce in a cup until smooth. Pour into the pan and simmer until the liquid has thickened. Garnish with the cilantro and cashew nuts. Serve hot with the rice.

SERVES 4 • PREPARATION 15 MIN. • COOKING 15 MIN. • LEVEL 1

9 pork & veggies
with polenta

Pork & Veggies
- 1 pound (500 g) pork loin, cut in small cubes
- 1¼ pounds (600 g) Savoy cabbage, cut into thin strips
- 1 small onion, thickly sliced
- 1 small carrot, sliced
- 1 stalk celery, sliced
- Dash of salt
- ½ cup (120 ml) hot water

Polenta
- 6 cups (1.5 liters) water
- 1⅓ cups (200 g) polenta (coarse-grain yellow cornmeal)
- 5 tablespoons (75 g) butter, cut into small pieces
- 4 tablespoons freshly grated Parmesan cheese
- Fresh rosemary sprigs, to garnish

Pork & Veggies Place the pork in a large, heavy-bottomed saucepan with the Savoy cabbage, onion, carrot, and celery. Add the salt and water. Cover tightly and bring quickly to a boil. Reduce the heat to low and simmer for 30 minutes.

Polenta While the pork and vegetables are cooking, bring 6 cups (1.5 liters) of salted water to a boil in a large, heavy-bottomed saucepan. Sprinkle in the polenta while stirring continuously with a large wooden spoon to prevent lumps from forming. Continue cooking over medium-low heat, stirring almost continuously, until the polenta starts to come away from the sides of the pan, 40–50 minutes.

Add the meat, vegetables, and their cooking liquid to the polenta and stir well. Simmer for 5–10 more minutes, stirring very frequently and adding a little boiling water when necessary to keep the polenta very moist and soft. Stir in the butter and Parmesan. Serve immediately, garnished with the rosemary.

SERVES 4 • PREPARATION 15 MIN. • COOKING 1 HR. • LEVEL 2

Polenta originally comes from northern Italy, where it was the staple food of poor country people for centuries. But by the last decade of the 20th century, polenta had become a gourmet food, served in upscale restaurants as a creamy base for delicious mushroom and meat sauces.

10 beef & spinach stir-fry

- 2 pounds (1 kg) beef tenderloin, cut into thin strips
- 5 tablespoons (75 ml) dark soy sauce
- 5 tablespoons (75 ml) apple juice
- 1 teaspoon red pepper flakes
- 2 cloves garlic, sliced
- 1 papaya (pawpaw), peeled and cut into small cubes
- 10 cherry tomatoes, halved
- 12 ounces (350 g) rice stick noodles
- 3 tablespoons peanut oil
- 2 stalks celery, sliced
- 2 tablespoons finely chopped fresh ginger
- 5 cups (250 g) baby spinach leaves

Combine the beef with the soy sauce, apple juice, red pepper flakes, garlic, papaya, and tomatoes in a large bowl. Mix well. Let marinate for 2 hours.

Cook the noodles according to the instructions on the package. Drain and set aside.

Heat the oil in a wok over high heat. Stir-fry the celery and ginger until aromatic, 1 minute. Add the beef and the marinade. Stir often until the liquid has evaporated and the meat is tender, about 5 minutes. Add the spinach and noodles. Stir-fry for 2 minutes. Serve hot.

SERVES 4–6 • PREPARATION 10 MIN. + 2 HR. TO MARINATE
COOKING 15 MIN. • LEVEL 2

11 spicy beef noodle stir-fry

- 14 ounces (400 g) ramen noodles
- 1 pound (500 g) lean beef fillet, cut into thin strips
- 2 tablespoons Asian chile oil
- 6 tablespoons (90 ml) freshly squeezed lemon juice
- 1 tablespoon soy sauce
- 2 cloves garlic, sliced
- 1 teaspoon grated ginger
- 1 teaspoon Tabasco
- 2 tablespoons peanut oil
- 1 onion, finely sliced
- 1 red bell pepper (capsicum), seeded and sliced
- 6 ounces (180 g) snow peas
- 1 cup (150 g) frozen corn
- 1 red chile, finely chopped
- 2 scallions (spring onions), sliced
- Cilantro (coriander) leaves

Cook the noodles according to the instructions on the package. Drain and set aside. Marinate the beef strips in the chile oil, 3 tablespoons of lemon juice, soy sauce, garlic, ginger, and Tabasco for 15 minutes.

Heat the oil in a wok over high heat. Add the onion and stir-fry until softened, 2–3 minutes. Add the beef mixture and stir-fry until lightly browned, 5–6 minutes. Add the bell pepper, snow peas, corn, chile, and remaining lemon juice. Stir-fry until the vegetables are crisp but tender, about 5 minutes. Add the scallions and noodles and stir-fry until heated. Serve hot with the cilantro.

SERVES 4 • PREPARATION 10 MIN. + 15 MIN. TO MARINATE • COOKING 15–20 MIN. • LEVEL 1

12 turkey breast in pancetta
with veggies

- 3 pounds (1.5 kg) turkey breast
- 2–3 tablespoons mixed chopped fresh sage, rosemary, and garlic
- Salt and freshly ground black pepper
- 12 ounces (350 g) pancetta, thinly sliced
- 1/4 cup (60 ml) extra-virgin olive oil
- 1 pound (500 g) white baby onions, peeled
- 2–3 carrots, sliced
- 1 pound (500 g) new potatoes, scraped
- 1 cup (250 ml) dry white wine
- 2 cups (500 ml) beef stock

Use a sharp knife to open the turkey breast out into a rectangular shape. Pound lightly with a meat tenderizer, taking care not to tear the meat. Sprinkle with the herb mixture, salt, and pepper.

Roll the meat up and sprinkle with a little more salt and pepper. Wrap the rolled turkey in the slices of pancetta so that it is completely covered and tie carefully with kitchen string.

Transfer to a heavy-bottomed saucepan and add the oil. Sauté over high heat, turning all the time, until the meat is evenly browned. After about 10 minutes, add the onions, carrots, and potatoes. Add the wine, decrease the heat, cover, and simmer until the meat and vegetables are tender and cooked, about 50 minutes, stirring from time to time. Add stock as required during cooking to keep the meat moist— the bottom of the pan should always be covered with liquid.

When cooked, untie the turkey, slice (not too thinly), and arrange on a serving dish with the vegetables. Serve hot with the cooking juices spooned over the top.

SERVES 4–6 • PREPARATION 30 MIN. • COOKING 1 HR. • LEVEL 2

13 pork & chorizo paella

- 1 pound (500 g) spinach
- ¼ cup (60 ml) extra-virgin olive oil
- 8 ounces (250 g) pork fillet, cut into bite-size pieces
- Salt and freshly ground black pepper
- 5 ounces (150 g) spicy chorizo, sliced
- 2 large red onions, chopped
- 1 green bell pepper (capsicum) and chopped
- 2 large tomatoes, sliced
- 3 large cloves garlic, sliced
- 2 cups (400 g) rice (Goya, Bomba, Arborio)
- 2 teaspoons sweet paprika
- 1 dried chile, crumbled
- 4 cups (1 liter) chicken stock
- Pinch of saffron threads, infused in 2 tablespoons of boiling water for 15 minutes

Cook the spinach in a boiling water until wilted, 2–3 minutes. Drain, chop coarsely, and set aside. Heat the oil in a large frying pan over high heat. Add the pork and sauté until browned, 3–5 minutes. Season with salt and pepper. Set aside. Sauté the chorizo in the pan until crisp, 3–4 minutes. Add the onions, bell pepper, tomatoes, and garlic and simmer for 20 minutes.

Add the rice, stirring to coat. Season with salt, pepper, and paprika. Add the chile, stock, and saffron liquid. Simmer for 15 minutes, until the stock is absorbed. Stir in the pork and spinach. Remove from the heat and let rest for 5 minutes. Serve hot.

SERVES 4–6 • PREPARATION 20 MIN. • COOKING 50 MIN. • LEVEL 2

14 arroz con pollo
(spanish rice with chicken)

- 4 pounds (2 kg) chicken pieces, with skin and bones
- Salt
- 1/4 cup (60 ml) vegetable oil
- 2 large onions, chopped
- 3 cloves garlic, sliced
- 1 red bell pepper (capsicum), seeded and diced
- 1/2 cup (60 g) diced ham
- 2 cups (400 g) rice
- 4 cups (1 liter) chicken stock
- 1/2 teaspoon saffron threads
- 1 cup (150 g) frozen mixed vegetables
- 1 small green chile, sliced
- 1/2 cup (60 g) black olives
- Fresh cilantro (coriander) and parsley

Season the chicken with salt. Heat the oil in a large frying pan over high heat. Add the chicken and sauté until browned, 8–10 minutes. Remove and set aside.

Add the onions, garlic, bell pepper, and ham. Sauté until softened, about 5 minutes. Add the rice and stock and bring to a boil. Return the chicken to the pan. Stir in the saffron. Cover and simmer on low heat for 20 minutes. Stir in the mixed vegetables, chile, and olives. Simmer until the rice is tender, about 10 minutes. Garnish with the cilantro and parsley and serve hot.

SERVES 6 • PREPARATION 20 MIN. • COOKING 45 MIN. • LEVEL 1

15 chicken meatballs
with veggies

- 1 eggplant (aubergine)
- Salt and freshly ground black pepper
- 8 tablespoons (120 ml) extra-virgin olive oil
- 1 clove garlic
- 1 large onion, thickly sliced
- 2 bell peppers (capsicums), red, yellow, or green, diced
- 1 zucchini (courgette), diced
- 10 cherry tomatoes, cut in half
- $\frac{1}{2}$ cup (50 g) black olives
- $1\frac{1}{4}$ pounds (600 g) ground chicken breast
- 2 tablespoons crustless bread, soaked in milk and squeezed
- $\frac{1}{2}$ cup (60 g) freshly grated Parmesan cheese
- 1 large egg
- 1 tablespoon finely chopped fresh parsley
- $\frac{1}{2}$ cup (75 g) all-purpose (plain) flour
- $\frac{1}{2}$ cup (120 ml) beef stock
- 10 leaves basil, torn

Cut the eggplant in thick slices, sprinkle with salt and place in a colander to drain for about 20 minutes. Cut into cubes.

Heat 4 tablespoons (60 ml) of oil in a large frying pan over medium heat. Add the garlic and onion and sauté until softened, 3–4 minutes. Add the bell peppers, eggplant, zucchini, tomatoes, and olives. Season with salt and pepper. Simmer until the vegetables are tender, about 20 minutes, adding a little water if the pan becomes too dry.

In the meantime, combine the chicken, bread, Parmesan, egg, parsley, and a little salt in a bowl and mix thoroughly. Shape the mixture into small round balls, then coat with flour.

Heat the remaining 4 tablespoons (60 ml) of oil in a large frying pan over medium heat. Fry the meatballs until golden brown all over, 5–7 minutes. Add the vegetable mixture, season with salt and pepper, and simmer for 5 minutes, stirring carefully. If the dish dries out too much, add stock as required.

Transfer to a heated serving dish, sprinkle with the basil and serve hot.

SERVES 6 • PREPARATION 20 MIN. + 20 MIN. TO DRAIN • COOKING 40 MIN. • LEVEL 2

16 lamb pilau

- 2 pounds (1 kg) boned lean lamb, cut in small cubes
- 2$\frac{1}{3}$ cups (620 ml) water
- 4 green cardamoms pods
- 2 black cardamom pods
- 12 black peppercorns
- 5 cloves
- 1 onion, sliced
- $\frac{1}{2}$ teaspoon salt
- 2 cups (400 g) basmati rice
- 1 teaspoon saffron threads
- 2 cloves garlic, finely chopped
- 2 teaspoons finely grated fresh ginger
- 1 short cinnamon stick
- 2 tablespoons butter
- 1 cup (150 g) almonds
- 1 cup (180 g) golden raisins (sultanas)

Place the lamb, water, both types of cardamom, peppercorns, cloves, onion, and salt in a medium pot and over medium heat and bring to a boil. Cover and simmer over low heat until the lamb is tender, about 30–40 minutes. Remove the lamb with a slotted spoon and set aside.

Strain the stock. Return to the pot and bring to a boil. Add the rice, saffron, garlic, ginger, cinnamon stick, and lamb. Simmer over low heat until the rice is cooked, 15–20 minutes. Top up with water if the rice absorbs all the water before it is cooked.

Melt the butter in a small frying pan over medium heat. Fry the almonds and raisins for 2–3 minutes. Spoon over the pilau and serve hot.

SERVES 4–6 • PREPARATION 20 MIN. • COOKING 50–60 MIN. • LEVEL 1

17 chicken biryani

- 4 tablespoons (60 g) ghee
- 2 large onions, thinly sliced
- 2 cloves garlic, sliced
- 1½ pounds (750 g) chicken thigh fillets, chopped
- 1 green chile, sliced
- 6 cardamom pods, bruised
- 2 teaspoons garam masala
- ½ teaspoon ground coriander
- ½ teaspoon cumin seeds
- ¼ teaspoon ground turmeric
- Salt and freshly ground black pepper
- 1½ cups (300 g) basmati rice
- 2 tomatoes, diced
- 3 tablespoons golden raisins (sultanas)
- 2 cups (500 ml) water
- ⅓ cup (50 g) cashews, lightly toasted
- 3 tablespoons chopped cilantro (coriander) + extra

Heat 2 tablespoons of ghee in a large frying pan over medium heat. Add the onions and garlic and sauté until softened, 3–4 minutes. Add the chicken and sauté until cooked through, 5–7 minutes. Set aside.

Heat the remaining ghee in a large saucepan over medium heat. Add the chile, cardamom, garam masala, coriander, cumin, turmeric, salt, and pepper, and cook until fragrant, about 30 seconds. Add the rice and stir to coat. Add the tomatoes, golden raisins, and water and bring to a boil. Decrease the heat and simmer, without stirring, for 5 minutes. Stir in the chicken mixture, cover, and simmer for 2 more minutes. Turn off the heat and set aside to finishing cooking, 10–15 minutes. Stir in the cashews and cilantro. Garnish with the extra cilantro and serve hot.

SERVES **4–6** • PREPARATION **20** MIN. • COOKING **25–30** MIN. • LEVEL **1**

18 roasted pork shanks
with mixed vegetables

- 3 pork shanks, about 3 pounds (1.5 kg) total weight
- 4 tablespoons all-purpose (plain) flour
- Salt and freshly ground black pepper
- 6 tablespoons (90 ml) extra-virgin olive oil
- 3/4 cup (200 ml) dry white wine
- 2 cups (500 ml) beef stock
- 2 large carrots, thickly sliced
- 2 stalks celery, thickly sliced
- 2 white onions, quartered
- 4 large potatoes, peeled and cut in chunks
- 2 zucchini (courgettes), thickly sliced

Preheat the oven to 400°F (200°C/gas 6). Roll the pork in the flour and season generously with salt and pepper. Heat 4 tablespoons (60 ml) of the oil in a large, heavy-bottomed pan, add the pork shanks and sauté over high heat until golden brown, 5–10 minutes. Transfer the shanks and their cooking juices to a roasting pan.

Roast for 20 minutes. Add the wine and roast for 40 minutes more, adding a little stock if the pan becomes too dry.

Meanwhile, heat the remaining 2 tablespoons of oil in a large heavy-bottomed pan over high heat and sauté the carrots, celery, onions, potatoes, and zucchini for 5–7 minutes.

When the shanks have been in the oven for about 1 hour, add the vegetables and their cooking juices. Return to the oven and roast for 1 hour more, basting with stock as required to stop the pan from drying out.

When cooked, arrange the meat and vegetables on a heated serving dish and serve hot.

SERVES 4–6 • PREPARATION 20 MIN. • COOKING 2 1/2 HR. • LEVEL 1

These roasted pork shanks and veggies make a wonderful Sunday lunch for family and friends. Serve with a glass of fine red wine and enjoy.

19 corned beef
with vegetables

- 6 pounds (3 kg) corned beef brisket
- 1 onion studded with 3 cloves
- 8 cloves garlic, peeled and left whole
- 1 tablespoon freshly ground black pepper
- 6 onions
- 6 potatoes
- 6 carrots
- $1/2$ teaspoon dried marjoram
- 6 turnips, peeled

Place the corned beef in an 8-quart (8-liter) pot. Pour in enough water to cover the beef completely. Bring to a boil over high heat and boil for 5 minutes. Skim off the froth from the surface. Add the onion with cloves, garlic, and pepper and boil for 10 minutes more.

Skim off any froth. Cover and simmer over very low heat for 1 hour. Add the onions and simmer for 30 minutes. Add the potatoes, carrots, turnips, and marjoram and simmer until all the vegetables are tender and the beef is cooked through, about 30 more minutes.

Remove the beef and discard the stock and the onion studded with cloves. Serve hot with the vegetables.

SERVES **8–10** • PREPARATION **20** MIN. • COOKING **2**$1/2$ HR. • LEVEL **1**

20 fillet steak
with spicy vegetables

- 1 pound (500 g) new potatoes, quartered
- 4 ounces (120 g) green beans
- 4 ounces (120 g) sugar snap peas (mangetout)
- 1 pound (500 g) fillet steak
- $^1/_2$ cup (120 ml) vegetable oil
- Salt and freshly ground black pepper
- $^1/_4$ cup (60 ml) red wine vinegar
- 1 clove garlic, finely chopped
- 2 teaspoons mustard
- 1 teaspoon sugar
- $^3/_4$ cup (75 g) green olives
- $^1/_2$ fresh red chile, seeded and finely chopped
- 1 tablespoon finely chopped fresh parsley
- 2 tomatoes, diced

Cook the potatoes in a large pot of boiling water until tender, 10–15 minutes. After 7 minutes, add the green beans and sugar snap peas. Cook until tender, 3–5 minutes. Drain well.

Sauté the steaks in 1 tablespoon of oil for 3–4 minutes on each side, until cooked to your liking. Season with salt and pepper. Slice the steak into thin strips.

Mix the remaining oil, red wine vinegar, garlic, mustard, and sugar in a small bowl. Arrange the steak, potatoes, green beans, sugar snap peas, olives, chile, parsley, and tomatoes in a large salad bowl. Drizzle with the dressing and toss gently. Serve hot.

SERVES 4 • PREPARATION 15 MIN. • COOKING 15–20 MIN. • LEVEL 1

thai chicken
pie
1

chicken & mushroom
pies
2

chicken, leek
& bacon pies
3

chicken filo parcels
4

chicken & feta pie
5

TOP
20

bastela
(moroccan chicken pie)
6

cottage pie
7

sausage & leek pie
8

beef & mushroom pies
9

pork & bacon pie
10

beef wellington pie
11

spicy shepherd's pie

downunder meat pies

steak pies

meat
pies

sausage & egg strudel

bacon, egg & veggie pie

beef & caramelized onion pie

lamb pasties

leek, pancetta & egg pies

cornish pasties

1 thai chicken pie

- 2 tablespoons sesame oil
- 2 onions, thinly sliced
- 2 red bell peppers (capsicums), seeded and diced
- $\frac{1}{4}$ cup (60 ml) Thai red curry paste
- 2 boneless skinless chicken breasts, cut into small cubes
- 1 (8-ounce/250-g) sheet ready-rolled puff pastry

Preheat the oven to 425°F (220°C/gas 7). Heat the oil in a large frying pan over medium heat. Add the onions, bell peppers, and red curry paste and sauté until softened, about 5 minutes. Add the chicken and sauté until cooked, about 5 minutes.

Spoon the filling into a deep 8-inch (20-cm) pie dish. Trim the pastry to fit the dish. Brush the edges of the pie dish with water and place the pastry on top. Press the edges down firmly to seal. Brush with a little water and prick all over with a fork. Bake for 25–30 minutes, until golden brown. Serve hot.

SERVES 4 • PREPARATION 15 MIN. • COOKING 35–40 MIN. • LEVEL 1

2 chicken & mushroom pies

- 2 boneless skinless chicken breasts, cut into small cubes
- 2 tablespoons extra-virgin olive oil
- 2 leeks, thinly sliced
- 8 ounces (250 g) mushrooms, quartered
- 1 cup (250 ml) sour cream
- 1 tablespoon Dijon mustard
- 2 tablespoons finely chopped fresh thyme
- Salt and freshly ground black pepper
- 1 (8-ounce/250-g) sheet ready-rolled puff pastry
- 1 large egg, lightly beaten

Preheat the oven to 425ºF (220ºC/gas 7). Heat the oil in a large frying pan over medium heat. Add the chicken and sauté until cooked, about 5 minutes. Add the leeks and mushrooms. Cover and simmer for 3 minutes. Stir in the sour cream, mustard, thyme, salt, and pepper. Spoon into four 1-cup (250-ml) ramekins.

Cut the pastry into four squares and place over the ramekins. Brush with the egg. Bake for 15 minutes, until puffed and golden. Serve hot.

SERVES 4 • PREPARATION 15 MIN. • COOKING 25 MIN. • LEVEL 1

3 chicken, leek & bacon pies

- 1 large chicken, about 4 pounds (2 kg)
- 2 carrots, chopped
- 3 onions, 1 halved, 2 finely chopped
- 1 bouquet garni, made of 1 stalk celery, 2 bay leaves, few sprigs each of fresh thyme and parsley, tied together with string
- 2 tablespoons extra-virgin olive oil
- 3 leeks, thickly sliced
- 12 ounces (350 g) smoked bacon lardons
- $\frac{2}{3}$ cup (150 g) butter
- 1 cup (150 g) all-purpose (plain) flour
- $\frac{1}{2}$ cup (120 ml) crème fraîche
- 2 tablespoons Dijon mustard
- Salt and freshly ground black pepper
- 1 large egg, beaten
- 2 (12-ounce/350-g) sheets ready-rolled puff pastry

Put the chicken in a large pot over high heat. Add the carrot, halved onion, and bouquet garni. Pour in enough cold water to cover. Bring to a boil, then simmer over low heat for 45 minutes.

Remove the chicken from the pot and set aside. Put the pot back over low heat and simmer until reduced. Remove the meat from the chicken and tear into bite-size pieces. Add the bones to the boiling stock. Simmer for 30 minutes. Strain the stock, discarding the solids. Measure out 6 cups (1.5 liters) of stock and set aside.

Heat the oil in a large saucepan over medium heat. Add the finely chopped onions and leeks and sauté until softened, about 5 minutes. Add the lardons and sauté until golden, about 5 minutes. Set aside.

Melt the butter in the same saucepan. Add the flour and stir until smooth. Gradually add the stock, stirring until smooth. Simmer for 2–3 minutes. Stir in the crème fraîche and mustard. Season with salt and pepper. Add the chicken and lardon mixture. Divide between two (8-cup/2-liter) oval pie dishes and let cool.

Preheat the oven to 400°F (200°C/gas 6). Brush the edges of the pie dishes with egg. Put the pastry on top, pressing down on the edges to seal. Make a small hole in each pie lid to let out steam. Brush with egg. Bake for 20–25 minutes until golden and bubbling. Serve hot.

SERVES 6–8 • PREPARATION 1 HR. • COOKING 2 HR. • LEVEL 2

4 chicken filo parcels

- 1 tablespoon sesame oil
- 3 shallots, finely chopped
- 2 cloves garlic, finely chopped
- 1 teaspoon finely grated fresh ginger
- 1 small red chile, seeded and finely chopped
- 4 ounces (120 g) shiitake mushrooms, finely diced
- 1 teaspoon Chinese 5-spice mix or pumpkin pie spice
- 1 pound (500 g) ground (minced) chicken
- 2 tablespoons light (single) cream
- 1 egg white, lightly beaten
- Salt
- 12 sheets filo (phyllo) pastry
- ½ cup (120 g) butter, melted

Heat the oil in a large frying pan over medium heat. Add the shallots, garlic, ginger, and chile and sauté until softened, 3–4 minutes. Add the mushrooms and spice mix and sauté until softened, about 5 minutes. Stir in the chicken, cream, and egg white. Season with salt.

Preheat the oven to 400°F (200 C/gas 6). Line two baking sheets with parchment paper. Layer three sheets of filo, brushing each one with melted butter. Cut into three strips lengthwise. Spoon a small amount of filling onto the end of each strip. Fold crosswise, in a back and forth motion, to create small triangular parcels. Repeat with the remaining filling. Arrange on the baking sheets. Bake for 15 minutes, until golden brown. Serve hot.

SERVES 6–8 • PREPARATION 30 MIN. • COOKING 25 MIN. • LEVEL 2

5 chicken & feta pie

- 2 tablespoons extra-virgin olive oil
- 1 large leek, thinly sliced
- 1 clove garlic, finely chopped
- 4 boneless skinless chicken breast halves, diced
- 1 bunch baby spinach leaves
- 3 grilled red bell peppers (capsicums), from a jar
- 1/2 cup (50 g) black olives
- 6 ounces (180 g) feta cheese, crumbled
- 2 tablespoons finely chopped fresh parsley
- 3 large eggs
- 1/4 cup (60 ml) heavy (double) cream
- 8 sheets filo (phyllo) pastry
- 1/3 cup (90 g) melted butter

Preheat the oven to 350°F (180°C/gas 4). Heat the oil in a large frying pan over medium heat. Add the leek, garlic, and chicken and sauté until the chicken is golden, about 5 minutes. Cook the spinach in a little salted water until just tender, 2–3 minutes. Drain well and chop coarsely. Mix the chicken, spinach, bell peppers, olives, feta, parsley, eggs, and cream in a bowl.

Butter a 9-inch (23-cm) square baking dish. Brush two sheets of filo lightly with butter. Place two more sheets on top and brush with butter. Line the baking dish with the filo. Fill with the chicken mixture. Brush the remaining filo with butter. Place on top of the pie. Brush with butter. Bake until golden, 40–45 minutes. Serve hot.

SERVES 4–6 • PREPARATION 45 MIN. • COOKING 55–60 MIN. • LEVEL 2

6 bastela
(moroccan chicken pie)

Pie

- 1 chicken, about 3 pounds (1.5 kg), quartered
- 2 large onions, chopped
- $^1/_2$ cup (120 ml) vegetable oil
- $^1/_4$ cup (60 g) butter, cubed
- 2 cloves garlic, bruised
- 2 teaspoons ground ginger
- 2 teaspoons salt
- 2 teaspoons turmeric
- 1 teaspoon freshly ground black pepper
- Pinch saffron threads
- $1^1/_4$ cups (300 ml) water
- 3 cups (150 g) coarsely chopped fresh parsley
- $^1/_2$ cup (25 g) coarsely chopped cilantro (coriander)
- 2 tablespoons freshly squeezed lemon juice
- $1^1/_2$ tablespoons sugar
- 1 teaspoon cinnamon + extra, to dust
- 10 large eggs, lightly beaten + 1 large egg yolk, to brush
- $^1/_2$ cup (120 g) butter, melted
- 10 sheets filo (phyllo) pastry
- Confectioners' (icing) sugar, to decorate

Almond Filling

- 3 tablespoons vegetable oil
- $2^1/_2$ cups (370 g) blanched almonds
- 2 tablespoons sugar

Pie Put the chicken, onions, oil, butter, garlic, ginger, salt, turmeric, pepper, and saffron in a large pot. Cover and simmer over low heat for 30 minutes. Add the water, cover, simmer until tender, about 45 minutes.

Almond Filling Heat the oil in a large frying pan over medium heat. Add the almonds and toss until golden brown. Drain on paper towels. Chop the almonds and sugar in a food processor to make fine crumbs.

Remove the chicken from the pan, reserving the liquid. Remove the meat and shred. Preheat the oven to 400°F (200°C/gas 6). Return the pan to the heat and bring the reserved liquid to a simmer. Add the parsley, cilantro, lemon juice, sugar, and cinnamon. Gradually add the eggs, stirring until thickened. Set aside.

Grease a 12-inch (30-cm) pan with butter. Brush nine filo sheets with butter and fold in half. Place a sheet in the pan. Top with the remaining sheets, overlapping, so that the pan is covered and there is an overhang to encase the filling. Drain any excess liquid off the egg mixture. Spread in the pastry case. Cover with the chicken and almond mixture. Wrap the pastry over the filling, brushing with melted butter. Brush the edges with egg yolk and lay the last sheet of filo on top. Brush with butter and egg yolk. Pierce a few holes in the top. Bake for 15–20 minutes, until golden brown. Dust with confectioners' sugar and decorate with cinnamon.

SERVES 6–8 • PREPARATION 1 HR. • COOKING 2 HR. • LEVEL 3

7 cottage pie

Pie
- 1 tablespoon extra-virgin olive oil
- 1 large onion, thinly sliced
- 2 carrots, cubed
- 1 1/4 pounds (600 g) ground (minced) beef
- 1 (14-ounce/400-g) can tomatoes, with juice
- 2 cups (500 ml) beef stock
- 1 bay leaf
- 1 tablespoon fresh thyme
- Freshly ground black pepper

Topping
- 2 pounds (1 kg) potatoes, peeled and cubed
- 4 tablespoons (60 g) butter
- 1/4 cup (60 ml) milk
- 2 teaspoons creamed horseradish

Pie Heat the oil in a large pan over medium heat. Add the onion and carrots and sauté until softened, 3–4 minutes. Add the beef and sauté browned, about 5 minutes. Add the tomatoes, beef stock, bay leaf, thyme, and pepper. Cover and simmer for 30 minutes.

Topping Cook the potatoes in salted boiling water until tender, about 10 minutes. Drain and mash with the butter and milk. Stir in the horseradish.

Preheat the oven to 375°F (190°C/gas 5). Spoon the meat into an ovenproof dish. Top with the mash and bake for 30 minutes, until golden brown. Serve hot.

SERVES 4 • PREPARATION 30 MIN. • COOKING 1 HR. • LEVEL 1

8   sausage & leek pies

- 8 good-quality, pork sausages, chopped
- 4 leeks, sliced
- 1 apple, peeled and sliced
- 1 tablespoon all-purpose (plain) flour
- 1 tablespoon grainy mustard
- 1 cup (250 ml) beef stock
- 1 (12-ounce/350-g) sheet ready-rolled puff pastry
- 1 egg, beaten

Preheat the oven to 400°F (200°C/gas 6). Sauté the sausages in a large frying pan over medium heat until browned, about 5 minutes. Set aside. Drain off most of the fat in the pan. Add the leeks and sauté until softened, 4–5 minutes. Add the apple. Stir in the flour, mustard, and stock and simmer until smooth, 1–2 minutes. Stir in the sausages.

Spoon into 4 ovenproof dishes or ramekins. Top with the pastry, trimming off any excess. Glaze with the egg. Bake for 25–30 minutes, until golden. Serve hot.

SERVES **4** • PREPARATION **15** MIN. • COOKING **35–40** MIN. • LEVEL **1**

9 beef & mushroom pies

- 2 tablespoons extra-virgin olive oil
- 1 pound (500 g) lean braising steak, cut into chunks
- 2 onions, thinly sliced
- 12 ounces (350 g) button mushrooms
- 1 clove garlic, finely chopped
- 1 tablespoon fresh thyme + extra sprigs, to garnish
- 1½ tablespoons all-purpose (plain) flour
- 1½ cups (370 ml) dry red wine
- Salt and freshly ground black pepper
- 1 (8-ounce/250-g) sheet ready-rolled puff pastry
- 1 large egg, beaten

Preheat the oven to 325°F (170°C/gas 3). Heat 1 tablespoon of oil in a large Dutch oven (casserole). Add the beef in two batches and brown all over, about 5 minutes each batch. Scoop the beef out with a slotted spoon and set aside.

Add the onions to the pan and sauté until just browned, 3–4 minutes. Scoop out the onions and set aside. Add the mushrooms and sauté until softened, about 5 minutes.

Return the beef and onions to the pan along with the garlic and thyme and sauté for 1 minute. Stir in the flour. Gradually add the wine, stirring constantly, and bring to a simmer. Season with salt and pepper. Cover, transfer to the oven, and bake for 2 hours, until the beef is very tender.

Take out of the oven. Increase the oven temperature to 375°F (190°C/gas 5). Divide the beef evenly among four small pie dishes. Cut the pastry into thin strips and use to make lattice-pattern tops for the pies. Brush with the egg to glaze.

Bake for 30 minutes, until the pastry is crisp and golden. Serve hot, garnished with a little extra thyme.

SERVES 4 • PREPARATION 30 MIN. • COOKING 3 HR. • LEVEL 2

10 pork & bacon pie

- 2 tablespoons vegetable oil
- 1 large onion, sliced
- 1 garlic clove, crushed
- 1 tablespoon fresh thyme
- 1½ pounds (750 g) pork loin, cubed
- 1 tablespoon butter
- 8 ounces (250 g) white mushrooms
- 1 tablespoon flour
- ½ cup (120 ml) chicken stock
- ½ cup (120 ml) heavy (double) cream
- Finely grated zest of 1 lemon
- Salt and freshly ground black pepper
- 1 (8-ounce/250-g) sheet ready-rolled puff pastry

Preheat the oven to 400°F (200°C/gas 6). Heat 1 tablespoon of oil in a large frying pan. Add the onion, garlic, and thyme and sauté until softened, 3–4 minutes. Transfer to a 5-cup (1.25-liter) ovenproof dish.

Heat 1 tablespoon of oil in the same pan over medium heat. Add the pork and sauté until browned, about 5 minutes. Add to the baking dish. Melt a knob of butter in the pan and cook the mushrooms until softened, about 5 minutes. Add to the baking dish. Mix in the flour. Whisk the chicken stock, cream, and lemon zest. Season with salt and pepper and pour into the dish.

Cover the dish with the pastry, trimming to fit. Bake for 30–40 minutes, until golden brown. Serve hot.

SERVES 4 • PREPARATION 15 MIN. • COOKING 45–55 MIN. • LEVEL 1

11 beef wellington pie

- 2 tablespoons vegetable oil
- 2 pounds (1 kg) braising steak, cut into chunks
- Salt and freshly ground black pepper
- 3 tablespoons flour
- 3 cups (750 ml) beef stock
- 1 tablespoon fresh thyme
- 2 tablespoons butter
- 2 shallots, finely chopped
- 2 cloves garlic, sliced
- 8 ounces (250 g) portobello mushrooms, finely chopped
- 3 tablespoons brandy
- 12 thin slices Parma ham
- 1 large egg, beaten
- 1 (14-ounce/400-g) sheet ready-rolled puff pastry

Heat the oil in a large saucepan over high heat. Season the beef with salt and pepper and sauté until browned, about 5 minutes. Add the flour, stock, and thyme. Cover, and simmer until very tender, 2–3 hours.

Preheat the oven to 400°F (200°C/gas 6). Melt the butter in a frying pan over medium heat. Add the shallots and garlic and sauté until softened, 3–4 minutes. Add the mushrooms and brandy and sauté until the pan is dry. Place a heaped teaspoon of mushroom on each slice of ham and roll up. Spoon the beef into a 6-cup (1.5-liter) pie dish. Add the ham rolls.

Brush the edge of the pie dish with beaten egg, cover with pastry, trim to fit, and cut an air vent. Bake for 45 minutes, until golden brown. Serve hot.

SERVES 4–6 • PREPARATION 15 MIN. • COOKING 45–55 MIN. • LEVEL 2

12 spicy shepherd's pie

- 6 medium potatoes, cut into chunks
- 2 tablespoons extra-virgin olive oil
- 1 large onion, finely sliced
- 1 pound (500 g) ground (minced) lamb
- 1 teaspoon crumbled dried chiles or red pepper flakes
- 3 tablespoons tomato paste (concentrate)
- 2–3 tablespoons Worcestershire sauce
- 3 tablespoons tomato ketchup
- Salt and freshly ground white pepper
- 1 tablespoon butter + extra, for the topping
- 3 tablespoons milk
- 1 tablespoon finely chopped fresh parsley, to garnish

Cook the potatoes in salted boiling water until very tender, about 20 minutes.

Heat the oil in a large frying pan over medium heat. Add the onion and sauté until softened, 3–4 minutes. Add the lamb and sauté over high heat until browned all over, 4–5 minutes.

Stir in the chiles, tomato paste, Worcestershire sauce, and tomato ketchup. Season with salt and white pepper, and simmer on low heat for 15 minutes.

Preheat the oven to 375°F (190°C/gas 5). Drain the potatoes and mash well with the butter and milk. Season with salt and pepper.

Spoon the lamb mixture into an ovenproof dish and top with the mashed potatoes. Dot with the extra butter. Bake for 25–30 minutes, until golden brown. Serve hot, garnished with the parsley.

SERVES 4 • PREPARATION 15 MIN. • COOKING 45–55 MIN. • LEVEL 1

Traditionally shepherd's pie was made with finely ground leftover roasted lamb. If you don't like spicy food, omit the chiles; the pie is equally good without them.

13 downunder meat pies

- 1 recipe pie crust
  (see page 250)
- 2 tablespoons vegetable oil
- 1 onion, finely chopped
- 1 pound (500 g) ground
  (minced) beef
- ³/₄ cup (180 ml) beef stock
- 1 tablespoon cornstarch
  (cornflour)
- 1 tablespoon Worcestershire
  sauce
- Salt and freshly ground
  pepper
- 1 small egg, lightly beaten
- Ketchup (tomato sauce),
  to serve

Prepare the pie crust. Heat the oil in a pan over medium heat. Add the onion and sauté until softened, 3–4 minutes. Add the beef and sauté until browned, 4–5 minutes. Add the stock, cornstarch, Worcestershire sauce, salt, and pepper and simmer until thickened.

Preheat the oven to 425°F (220°C/gas 7). Grease four 5-inch (13-cm) pie pans. Roll the dough out on a work surface to ⅛ inch (3 mm) thick. Cut out four pastry rounds. Line the bases and sides of the pans. Cut out four slightly larger lids and set aside.

Fill the pies with the filling. Brush the edges with water and cover with the lids. Press the edges with a fork to seal. Make small holes in the center of each pie. Brush with egg. Bake for 20–25 minutes, until the pastry is puffed and golden brown. Serve hot with ketchup.

SERVES 4 • PREPARATION 1 HR. • COOKING 35–40 MIN. • LEVEL 2

14 steak pies

- 1 recipe pie crust (see page 250)
- 2 tablespoons vegetable oil
- 2 onions, finely chopped
- 3 garlic cloves, finely chopped
- 1½ pounds (750 g) braising steak, cut into small chunks
- 2 tablespoons all-purpose (plain) flour
- Salt and freshly ground black pepper
- 3 sprigs of fresh thyme
- 1 fresh bay leaf
- 1½ cups (375 ml) dark ale
- 1 cup (250 ml) beef stock
- 2 teaspoons English mustard
- 2 tablespoons Worcestershire sauce
- Ketchup (tomato sauce), to serve

Prepare the pie crust. Heat the oil in a large pan over medium heat and sauté the onion and garlic until softened, 3–4 minutes. Toss the steak in the flour and season with salt and pepper. Add to the pan and sauté until browned, 5–8 minutes. Add the thyme, bay leaf, ale, stock, mustard, and Worcestershire sauce. Simmer until the meat is tender, about 2 hours. Discard the bay leaf and thyme.

Preheat the oven to 425°F (220°C/gas 7). Prepare the pies following the instructions for the meat pies on the facing page. Bake for 20–25 minutes, until the pastry is puffed and golden brown. Serve hot with ketchup.

SERVES 4 • PREPARATION 1 HR. • COOKING 2½ HR. • LEVEL 2

15 sausage & egg strudel

Pie Crust
- 1 cup (250 g) salted butter, chilled and diced
- 3⅓ cups (500 g) all-purpose (plain) flour
- 1 large egg, beaten

Strudel
- 5 large eggs
- 1½ pounds (750 g) good-quality pork sausages, peeled and crumbled
- 2 dessert apples, peeled, cored, and grated
- 4 scallions (spring onions), finely chopped
- 2 tablespoons finely chopped fresh parsley
- 2 tablespoons finely chopped fresh chives
- 3 tablespoons crème fraîche or plain yogurt
- 1 tablespoon wholegrain mustard
- 1 cup (150 g) fine dry bread crumbs
- ½ cup (60 g) freshly grated mature Cheddar cheese
- Salt and freshly ground black pepper
- 2 (14-ounce/400-g) sheets ready-rolled puff pastry

Pie Crust Rub the butter into the flour. Stir in the egg to make a firm dough. Wrap in plastic wrap (cling film) and chill for 30 minutes.

Strudel Preheat the oven to 400°F (200°C/gas 6). Place 4 eggs in a pan of cold water and bring to a boil. Simmer gently until soft-boiled, about 3 minutes. Let cool, then shell and set aside.

Put the sausage meat in a bowl. Add the apples, scallions, parsley, chives, crème fraîche, mustard, bread crumbs, and cheese. Season with salt and pepper.

Roll out half the pastry on a floured work surface. Cut out a rectangle, measuring about 6 x 12 inches (15 x 30 cm). Arrange half the sausage filling down the center of the pastry, leaving a 2-inch (5-cm) border. Top with the whole peeled eggs in a row, lengthwise. Cover with the remaining filling.

Whisk the remaining egg in a bowl. Brush some over the edges of the pastry. Roll out the remaining pastry into a sheet large enough to drape over the sausage filling. Press down well on the edges to seal in the filling. Trim the pastry and crimp the edges with a fork. Brush with the egg and make several slashes in the top to release steam. Bake for about 1 hour, until golden brown. Serve hot.

SERVES 4–6 • PREPARATION 30 MIN. + 30 MIN. TO CHILL • COOKING 1 HR. • LEVEL 2

16 bacon, egg & veggie pie

- 1 tablespoon extra-virgin olive oil
- 1 large onion, sliced
- 6 thick slices bacon, rinds removed
- 1 pound (500 g) new potatoes, halved
- 20 cherry tomatoes, halved
- 1 cup (150 g) frozen peas
- 2 tablespoons coarsely chopped fresh parsley
- 8 large eggs
- ½ cup (120 ml) heavy (double) cream
- Salt and freshly ground black pepper

Preheat the oven to 400°F (200°C/gas 6). Heat the oil in a large frying pan over medium heat. Sauté the onion until softened, 3–4 minutes. Add the bacon and sauté until crisp, 3–4 minutes.

Cook the potatoes in boiling water for 5 minutes. Drain. Combine the potatoes and the onion and bacon mixture in a medium roasting pan lined with baking paper. Top with the tomatoes, peas, and parsley. Whisk the eggs and cream and season with salt and pepper. Pour into the pan. Bake for 20 minutes until just set and golden. Lift out of the pan using the baking paper and serve hot.

SERVES 4 • PREPARATION 15 MIN. • COOKING 35–40 MIN. • LEVEL 2

17 beef & caramelized onion pie

- $\frac{1}{4}$ cup (30 g) + 1 tablespoon all-purpose (plain) flour
- Salt and freshly ground black pepper
- 2 pounds (1 kg) chuck steak, cut into bite-size chunks
- 3 tablespoons vegetable oil
- 2 tablespoons butter
- 4 cloves garlic, crushed
- 8 ounces (250 g) button mushrooms
- 3 large onions, sliced
- 1 tablespoon sugar
- 1 cup (250 ml) beef stock
- 1$\frac{1}{2}$ cups (370 ml) brown ale
- 1 teaspoon tomato paste (concentrate)
- Few sprigs fresh thyme
- 3 tablespoons Worcestershire sauce
- 1 (8-ounce/250-g) ready-rolled puff pastry sheet

Season the flour with salt and pepper. Dust over the beef. Heat 2 tablespoons of oil in a large pan over high heat. Add the beef and sauté until browned. Set aside. Add the butter, garlic, and mushrooms to the pan and sauté for 2 minutes. Set aside. Heat the remaining oil in the pan over low heat. Add the onions and sugar and simmer until caramelized, 20–30 minutes. Stir in 1 tablespoon of flour, stock, ale, tomato paste, thyme, Worcestershire sauce, beef, and mushrooms. Cover and simmer until the beef is tender, about 1$\frac{1}{2}$ hours.

Preheat the oven to 450°F (230°C/gas 8). Spoon the filling into a 8-cup (2-liter) oval pie dish. Lay the pastry over the top. Trim and cut a hole for steam to escape. Bake for 15 minutes, until golden. Serve hot.

SERVES 4–6 • PREPARATION 25 MIN. • COOKING 2$\frac{1}{4}$ HR. • LEVEL 2

18 lamb pasties

- 2 tablespoons all-purpose (plain) flour
- Salt and freshly ground black pepper
- 4 lamb shanks
- 2 tablespoons butter
- 2 leeks, sliced
- 2 carrots, diced
- 2 small turnips, diced
- 1 bay leaf
- 1 teaspoon tomato paste (concentrate)
- 1 tablespoon white wine vinegar
- 5 cups (1.25 liters) chicken stock, hot
- Small bunch of fresh mint, chopped
- 2 (1-pound/500-g) sheets ready-rolled puff pastry
- 1 large egg, beaten
- English pickle or chutney, to serve

Put the flour in a shallow bowl, season with salt and pepper, and add the lamb. Turn to coat. Heat the butter in a large casserole over medium heat and brown the shanks all over, 5–10 minutes. Remove and set aside.

Stir the leeks, carrots, and turnips into the butter and juices in the pan. Add the bay leaf, tomato paste, and vinegar and mix well. Return the lamb to the casserole and pour in the stock. Cover and simmer for at least 2 hours, until the meat is falling off the bone. Check the seasoning. Allow the casserole to cool. Strain the liquid and discard, then cut the meat into chunky pieces. Put in a bowl and mix with the vegetables and mint.

Preheat the oven to 350°F (180°C/gas 4). Line a large baking sheet with parchment paper. Cut out four 8-inch (20-cm) circles from each sheet of pastry. Brush the bases with egg. Divide the filling mixture evenly among the pastry circles. Pull the sides up around the filling and crimp the pastry at the join. Brush with egg.

Transfer to the prepared baking sheet. Bake for 30–45 minutes, until golden brown. Serve hot with pickle or chutney.

SERVES **4–8** • PREPARATION **15** MIN. • COOKING **3** HR. • LEVEL **2**

19 leek, pancetta & egg pies

- 2 tablespoons extra-virgin olive oil
- 2 leeks, thinly sliced
- 8 ounces (250 g) pancetta slices, chopped
- 10 large eggs
- ½ cup (120 ml) light (single) cream
- 1 tablespoon wholegrain mustard
- Salt and freshly ground black pepper

Preheat the oven to 350°F (180°C/gas 4). Grease six ¾-cup (180-ml) ramekins with oil.

Heat the oil in a large frying pan over medium heat. Add the leeks and sauté until softened, 3–4 minutes. Meanwhile, beat 4 eggs with the cream and mustard in a medium bowl. Season with salt and pepper. Stir in the leek mixture. Mix well.

Spoon the mixture into the prepared ramekins. Crack one egg into each ramekin. Bake for 15–20 minutes, until golden and set. Let cool in the ramekins for 5 minutes. Turn out onto racks. Serve hot.

SERVES 6 • PREPARATION 15 MIN. • COOKING 20–25 MIN. • LEVEL 1

20 cornish pasties

- 1 recipe pie crust
  (see page 250)
- 1 pound (500 g) chuck
  steak, finely chopped with
  a large knife
- 1 large onion, finely chopped
- 2 medium potatoes, peeled
  and cut in small cubes
- 2 cups (300 g) frozen mixed
  vegetables
- 1 teaspoon salt
- 1 teaspoon freshly ground
  black pepper

Prepare the pie crust. Preheat the oven to 400°F (200°C/gas 6). Line a baking sheet with parchment paper. Mix the steak, onion, potatoes, mixed vegetables, salt, and pepper in a bowl. Roll out the dough on a lightly floured work surface to very thin. Cut out four 9-inch (23-cm) circles. Place a quarter of the filling along the center of each circle. Brush the edges with the egg. Draw up the sides to meet at the top. Pinch to seal.

Transfer to the baking sheet. Bake for 10 minutes, then lower oven temperature to 350°F (180°C/gas 4) and bake for 45 minutes, until golden. Serve hot.

SERVES 4 • PREPARATION 45 MIN. • COOKING 55–60 MIN. • LEVEL 2

duck & fig
tagine

chicken noisettes
with pesto filling

spring chicken
baked in coarse sea salt

roast duck
with olives & sherry

roast guinea fowl
with rosemary & lemon

TOP
20

stuffed chicken legs
with truffles & parmesan mash

tuscan fried chicken

battered fried chicken

tuscan chicken pot roast

chinese pork rolls
with apple

pork medallions
with winter fruit

12
roast turkey
with pomegranate

13
lamb tagine
with dates

14
roast pork
with walnut sauce

special
occasions

15
roast suckling pork
with vegetables

16
pork chops
with poached quinces

17
pork chops
with gremolata

18
sicilian stuffed veal roll

19
beef steaks with sweet potatoes
& mushrooms

20
rib of lamb
with garlic mash

1 duck & fig tagine

- ⅓ cup (90 g) butter
- 1 duck, weighing about 4 pounds (2 kg), cut into 8–10 pieces
- 2 onions, finely chopped
- 2 cloves garlic, finely chopped
- 1 teaspoon finely chopped fresh ginger
- 1 teaspoon ground turmeric
- Salt
- 1½ cups (370 ml) water
- 2 tablespoons honey
- 1 teaspoon ground cinnamon
- 1¾ pounds (800 g) fresh figs, quartered
- Fresh basil leaves to garnish

Melt the butter in a tagine or heavy-based saucepan over medium heat. Add the duck, onions, and garlic and sauté until nicely browned, 8–10 minutes. Add the ginger, turmeric, and salt. Pour in the water. Cover and simmer over very low heat until the duck is tender, 40–45 minutes.

Add the honey and cinnamon and simmer for 10 minutes. Stir in the figs and cook for 5 more minutes. Garnish with the mint or basil and serve hot.

SERVES 6 • PREPARATION 15 MIN. • COOKING 65–70 MIN. • LEVEL 2

2 chicken noisettes
with pesto filling

Chicken Noisettes

- 4 slices bacon
- 4 boneless skinless chicken breast halves
- 1 tablespoon freshly squeezed lemon juice
- Salt and freshly ground black pepper
- 2 tablespoons melted butter

Pesto Filling

- 1 cup (60 g) fresh bread crumbs
- 1 clove garlic
- $1/4$ cup (45 g) pine nuts
- 1 tablespoon freshly squeezed lemon juice
- $1/4$ cup (60 ml) extra-virgin olive oil
- Salt and freshly ground black pepper
- 1 small bunch fresh parsley or basil
- Steamed vegetables, to serve

Chicken Noisettes Preheat the oven to 350°F (180°C/gas 4). Trim the slices of bacon to the same size as the chicken breasts. Reserve the trimmings. Gently flatten the chicken with a meat tenderizer. Drizzle with the lemon juice and season with salt and pepper.

Pesto Filling Combine all the filling ingredients and bacon trimmings in a food processor and chop until smooth. Spread each chicken breast with a quarter of the filling and roll up. Wrap a bacon slice around each noisette, overlapping the ends. Insert a wooden skewer through the overlap and the center of each noisette. Butter a baking dish. Place the noisettes in the dish and brush with melted butter. Bake until golden brown, about 30 minutes. Slice and serve hot with vegetables.

SERVES 4–6 • PREPARATION 20 MIN. • COOKING 30 MIN. • LEVEL 2

3 spring chicken
baked in coarse sea salt

- 10 pounds (5 kg) coarse sea salt
- 3 sprigs fresh sage
- 3 sprigs fresh rosemary
- 3 cloves garlic, whole
- 1 chicken, about 3–4 pounds (1.5–2 kg)

Preheat the oven to 375°F (190°C/gas 5). Spread 3 pounds (1.5 kg) of coarse salt on the bottom of a high-sided baking dish.

Tie the herbs together and insert in the abdominal cavity of the chicken with the garlic.

Place the chicken in the baking dish and cover with the rest of the salt. No parts of the chicken should be visible.

Bake for 1½ hours. The salt will form a firm crust. Take out of the oven and bring to the table in the baking dish. Break the crust and remove the chicken. Carve and serve hot.

SERVES 4 • PREPARATION 10 MIN. • COOKING 1½ HR. • LEVEL 1

Cooking meat or fish in salt enhances its taste. A crisp, salty crust forms on the outside, which can be nibbled on or discarded, as preferred, while the inside stays moist and tender. Surprisingly, in view of the cooking method, the meat is not at all salty.

4 roast duck
with olives & sherry

- ½ cup (50 g) large green olives, pitted and sliced
- 1 (5-pound/2.5-kg) duck, as much fat removed as possible
- Salt and freshly ground black pepper
- 1 onion, coarsely chopped
- 2 carrots, coarsely chopped
- 3 cloves garlic, finely chopped
- 1 tablespoon extra-virgin olive oil
- ¾ cup (180 ml) chicken stock
- ¼ cup (60 ml) dry white wine or sherry
- ¾ teaspoon dried thyme
- 1 tablespoon finely chopped fresh parsley

Preheat the oven to 350ºF (180ºC/gas 4). Soak the olives in warm water in a small bowl. Season the duck inside and out with salt and pepper. Truss the duck with kitchen string. Place in a roasting pan and prick all over with a fork. Roast for 1 hour.

Sauté the onion, carrots, and garlic in the oil in a Dutch oven over medium heat until softened, 5–10 minutes. Carve the duck and place in the Dutch oven. Pour off the fat in the roasting pan and deglaze with the chicken stock, scraping up any brown bits. Strain into the Dutch oven. Drain the olives and stir in with the wine, thyme, and parsley. Season with salt and pepper. Cover and bake until very tender, about 1 hour. Serve hot.

SERVES 4 • PREPARATION 30 MIN. • COOKING 2¼ HR. • LEVEL 2

5 roast guinea fowl
with rosemary & lemon

- ¼ cup (60 ml) extra-virgin olive oil
- 2 tablespoons freshly squeezed lemon juice
- 1 tablespoon coarsely chopped fresh rosemary
- 1 clove garlic, finely chopped
- Salt and freshly ground black pepper
- 2 guinea fowl, cut in half
- Roasted potatoes, to serve

Mix the oil, lemon juice, rosemary, and garlic in a small bowl. Season with salt and pepper. Place the guinea fowl in a large bowl and pour in the marinade. Turn well to coat. Chill for 4 hours.

Preheat the oven to 350°F (180°C/gas 4). Place the birds on a rack in a roasting pan. Roast until tender and cooked through, about 1 hour. Baste with the marinade every 15 minutes during roasting. Serve hot.

SERVES 4 • PREPARATION 10 MIN. + 4 HR. TO MARINATE • COOKING 1 HR. • LEVEL 2

6 stuffed chicken legs
with truffles & parmesan mash

- 4 large chicken legs
- 1 pound (500 g) Italian pork sausages, peeled and crumbled
- Black truffles, cut in tiny cubes (optional)
- 5 tablespoons (75 g) butter
- 3–4 sprigs rosemary
- Salt and freshly ground black pepper
- $1\frac{1}{2}$ pounds (750 g) potatoes, peeled
- $\frac{1}{2}$ cup (60 g) freshly grated Parmesan cheese
- 3 tablespoons milk

Preheat the oven to 350°F (180°C/gas 4). Use a sharp knife to open the chicken legs up and remove the bone. Leave the bottom bone in to be used as a handle.

Place the sausage meat and truffles, if using, in a bowl and mix well. Stuff the chicken legs with this mixture. Tie with kitchen string.

Place the stuffed chicken legs in a baking dish with 3 tablespoons of butter and the rosemary. Season with salt and pepper and bake until tender, about 40 minutes.

Meanwhile, cook the potatoes in a pot of salted boiling water until tender. Drain and mash well, adding the remaining 2 tablespoons of butter, cheese, and milk.

Serve the chicken hot with the mashed potatoes.

SERVES 4 · PREPARATION 30 MIN. · COOKING 40 MIN. · LEVEL 3

If preferred, ask your butcher to de-bone the chicken legs. This is an Italian recipe, but if you can't find Italian pork sausages, replace with any good-quality local, highly flavored pork sausages.

7 tuscan fried chicken

- 3 pounds (1.5 kg) chicken pieces
- 3 tablespoons finely chopped fresh parsley
- Freshly squeezed juice of 1 lemon
- 3 tablespoons extra-virgin olive oil
- Salt and freshly ground black pepper
- 2 large eggs
- 2 cups (500 ml) sunflower oil, for frying
- 2 tablespoons all-purpose (plain) flour

Put the chicken in a bowl with the parsley. Add the lemon juice and olive oil. Season with salt and pepper. Cover and marinate in the refrigerator for 2 hours.

Beat the eggs in a bowl. Heat the sunflower oil in a large frying pan over medium-high heat. Drain the chicken. Dredge in the flour, ensuring that it is evenly coated. Shake to remove any excess flour.

Dip each piece of chicken in the beaten egg. Fry in batches in the oil until cooked and golden brown, 10–15 minutes. Drain on paper towels and serve hot.

SERVES 4–6 • PREPARATION 15 MIN. + 2 HR. TO MARINATE • COOKING 20–30 MIN. • LEVEL 2

8 battered fried chicken

- 3 pounds (1.5 kg) chicken pieces
- Salt and freshly ground black pepper
- Freshly squeezed juice of 3 lemons
- ½ cup (75 g) all-purpose (plain) flour
- 2 eggs, lightly beaten
- 2 cloves garlic, peeled but whole
- 2 cups (500 ml) olive oil, for frying

Season the chicken with salt and pepper. Place in a large bowl and drizzle with the lemon juice. Cover and marinate in the refrigerator for 2 hours.

Squeeze the pieces of marinated chicken to remove excess lemon juice. Dip in the flour and then in the egg.

Fry the garlic in the oil in a large, deep frying pan until pale gold. Discard the garlic. Fry the chicken in batches in the oil until cooked and golden brown, 10–15 minutes. Drain on paper towels and serve hot.

SERVES 4–6 • PREPARATION 15 MIN. + 2 HR. TO MARINATE • COOKING 20–30 MIN. • LEVEL 2

9 tuscan chicken pot roast

- 3 ounces (90 g) pancetta, sliced thinly
- 2 sprigs of rosemary
- 1 whole chicken, weighing about 4 pounds (2 kg)
- Salt and freshly ground black pepper
- 2 ounces (60 g) fatty prosciutto, chopped
- 2 cloves garlic, finely chopped
- $1/3$ cup (90 ml) stock + extra, as required
- 1 tablespoon white wine vinegar
- $1^{1}/_{2}$ pounds (750 g) potatoes, cut into chunks

Insert the strips of pancetta and the rosemary into the cavity of the chicken. Season with salt and pepper.

Heat a large Dutch oven or casserole over medium heat. Sauté the prosciutto and garlic until lightly browned, about 5 minutes. Add the chicken.

Add the stock and vinegar and bring to a boil. Cover and simmer over low heat for 1 hour. Remove the lid and add the potatoes and a little more stock to stop the chicken from sticking. Cover and cook until the potatoes are tender, 35–40 minutes. Serve hot.

SERVES **4–6** • PREPARATION **15** MIN. • COOKING **1**^{3}/**4** HR. • LEVEL **2**

Roasting meat in a pot on the stovetop is a tradition in Tuscany. Up until the second half of the 20th century, many homes did not have an oven.

10 chinese pork rolls
with apple

- 2 apples, peeled, cored, and coarsely chopped
- $1/2$ cup (90 g) golden raisins (sultanas)
- Freshly squeezed juice of $1/2$ lemon
- 2 pounds (1 kg) pork tenderloin, cut in $1/4$-inch (5-mm) thick slices
- $1/2$ cup (120 ml) Chinese plum sauce
- $1/2$ cup (120 ml) apple juice
- 1 tablespoon light soy sauce
- 1 tablespoon honey
- Steamed snow peas (mangetout), to serve

Preheat the oven to 350°F (180°C/gas 4). Mix the apples, golden raisins, and lemon juice in a small bowl. Spread each pork slice with the plum sauce. Place a small amount of the apple mixture in the center. Roll up and tie with kitchen string. Place the pork rolls in a baking dish seam-side down.

Mix the apple juice, soy sauce, and honey in a small bowl and pour over the pork. Cover with aluminum foil. Bake until tender, 20–25 minutes. Serve hot with the snow peas.

SERVES 6–8 • PREPARATION 20 MIN. • COOKING 20–25 MIN. • LEVEL 2

11 pork medallions
with winter fruit

- 1 apple, peeled, cored, and diced
- 1 pear, peeled, cored, and diced
- $\frac{1}{2}$ cup (120 ml) dry white wine
- $\frac{1}{2}$ cup (120 ml) chicken stock
- $3\frac{1}{2}$ ounces (100 g) dried fruit such as apricots, peaches, pears, and prunes
- 1 teaspoon ground cinnamon
- 1 tablespoon extra-virgin olive oil
- 1 pound (500 g) pork tenderloin, cut into $\frac{1}{4}$-inch (5-mm) thick medallions
- 2 tablespoons brandy

Combine the apple, pear, wine, and chicken stock in a saucepan. Bring to a boil. Simmer over low heat until the fruit has softened, about 10 minutes. Add the dried fruit and cinnamon. Simmer until the fruit is plump, about 30 minutes. Remove from the heat.

Heat the oil in a large frying pan over medium heat. Add the pork and fry until browned, about 5 minutes. Set aside. Turn up the heat. Add the brandy and let it evaporate. Add a little of the cooking liquid from the fruit. Cook over medium heat, stirring constantly, to deglaze the pan. Stir in the fruit mixture and cook until heated through, about 2 minutes. Return the pork to the pan. Cook, stirring occasionally, until tender and cooked through, about 5 minutes. Serve hot.

SERVES 4 • PREPARATION 20 MIN. • COOKING 50 MIN. • LEVEL 2

12 roast turkey
with pomegranate

- 1 young, tender turkey, 4–5 pounds (2 kg), with liver (separate from the bird)
- Salt and freshly ground black pepper
- 4 tablespoons (60 g) butter
- 9 tablespoons (135 ml) extra-virgin olive oil
- 4 fresh sage leaves, finely chopped
- 3 whole ripe pomegranates
- Steamed or boiled new potatoes, to serve

Preheat the oven to 350°F (180°C/gas 4). Season the cavity of the turkey with salt and pepper and put 2 tablespoons of butter inside. Tie up the turkey so that the legs and wings sit snugly against its sides.

Place the turkey in a fairly deep roasting pan or ovenproof dish. Smear with the remaining 2 tablespoons of butter, drizzle with 8 tablespoons (120 ml) of oil, and sprinkle with the sage. Roast for 3 hours. Baste the turkey with its own juices at intervals as it cooks.

Place the seeds of 2 of the pomegranates in a blender and process to obtain a smooth juice. After the turkey has been in the oven for 1½ hours, drizzle with half the pomegranate juice.

Rinse and trim the liver. Chop coarsely and fry in the remaining 1 tablespoon of oil over high heat. Add the remaining pomegranate juice, season with salt and pepper, and remove from the heat.

When the turkey is done, cut into 10–12 pieces. Place in an ovenproof dish and pour the liver and pomegranate sauce over the top. Sprinkle with the seeds of the remaining pomegranate and roast for 10 more minutes before serving.

SERVES 8–10 • PREPARATION 30 MIN. • COOKING 3¼ HR. • LEVEL 2

13 lamb tagine
with dates

- $\frac{1}{3}$ cup (90 g) butter
- 4 pounds (2 kg) boneless leg of lamb, diced
- 5 onions, finely chopped
- 2 cloves garlic, finely chopped
- 1 teaspoon ground ginger
- 1 teaspoon ground turmeric
- Pinch of salt
- $1\frac{1}{2}$ cups (370 ml) water
- 2 pounds (1 kg) pitted dates
- 3 tablespoons honey
- 1 teaspoon ground cinnamon
- 1 tablespoon sesame seeds
- 1 tablespoon slivered almonds
- 1 tablespoon coarsely chopped fresh parsley

Melt the butter in a large saucepan over medium heat. Sauté the lamb, onions, and garlic until lightly browned, 8–10 minutes. Add the ginger, turmeric, and salt. Pour in the water. Cover and simmer over low heat until the lamb is tender, 35–40 minutes.

Stir in the dates, honey, and cinnamon. Uncover and cook until the sauce has reduced, 12–15 minutes. Sprinkle with the sesame seeds, slivered almonds, and parsley. Serve hot.

SERVES **6–8** • PREPARATION **20** MIN. • COOKING **60–65** MIN. • LEVEL **2**

14 roast pork
with walnut sauce

- 3 pounds (1.5 kg) pork tenderloin
- Salt and freshly ground black pepper
- 1 tablespoon butter
- Freshly grated nutmeg
- 1 tablespoon brandy
- 4 cups (1 liter) milk + more, if needed
- 5 ounces (150 g) walnuts
- Mashed potatoes, to serve
- Baked apples, to serve

Preheat the oven to 400°F (200°C/gas 6). Season the pork with salt, pepper, and nutmeg, and rub with butter. Season with nutmeg. Heat a large frying pan over high heat. Brown the pork on all sides. Add the brandy, tilting the pan to ignite it. Let it burn out.

Transfer the pork to a small, deep baking dish. Cover with milk and bake until tender, about 2 hours. After 1 hour, add the walnuts. Season with salt and pepper. Add more milk to keep the meat moist. Serve hot with the potatoes and apples and drizzled with the sauce.

SERVES **6–8** • PREPARATION **15** MIN. **+ 1** HR TO REST • COOKING **2** HR. • LEVEL **2**

15 roast suckling pork
with vegetables

- 6 tablespoons (90 ml) extra-virgin olive oil
- 2 onions, quartered
- 2 carrots, thickly sliced
- 2 stalks celery, thickly sliced
- 2 zucchini (courgettes), thickly sliced
- 4 potatoes, quartered
- 1 leek, thickly sliced
- Salt
- ½ suckling pig, about 4 pounds (2 kg)
- 10 peppercorns
- 2 bay leaves
- ¾ cup (200 ml) dry white wine
- 1 tablespoon finely chopped garlic and parsley

Preheat the oven to 400° (200°C/gas 6). Heat 4 tablespoons of oil in a large, heavy-bottomed pan over high heat. Add the onions, carrots, celery, zucchini, potatoes, and leek and sauté until pale golden brown, 8–10 minutes. Sprinkle with salt. Remove from the heat and set aside.

Add the remaining 2 tablespoons of oil to the same pan and brown the pork, 5–10 minutes. Transfer the meat and any liquid it has produced to a roasting pan. Sprinkle with a little more salt and the peppercorns. Add the bay leaves and turn the meat in its juices.

Roast for about 1½ hours, basting frequently and gradually adding the wine. When the pork has been in the oven for 45 minutes, add the vegetables and sprinkle with the garlic and parsley. When the meat is cooked, it will have a dark, crisp layer of crackling.

Arrange on a heated serving dish with the vegetables and serve hot.

SERVES 6–8 • PREPARATION 15 MIN. • COOKING 2 HR. • LEVEL 2

Suckling pork is butchered when the pig is between two and six weeks old. The meat is pale and very tender and the cooked skin is crisp. You can also use meat from an older animal in this recipe.

16 pork chops
with poached quinces

- 3 tablespoons (45 ml) extra-virgin olive oil
- 4 pork loin chops, bone-in
- 1 onion, thinly sliced
- 1 clove garlic, finely chopped
- 1 medium quince, peeled, cored, and cut into thin wedges
- $\frac{1}{2}$ cup (120 ml) dry white wine
- Freshly squeezed juice of 1 orange
- $\frac{1}{3}$ cup (90 ml) chicken stock
- 2-inch (5-cm) long cinnamon stick
- 1 tablespoon honey
- 1 tablespoon finely chopped fresh parsley
- Salt and freshly ground black pepper

Heat 1 tablespoon of oil in a large frying pan over high heat. Add the chops and sear for 2 minutes on each side. Set aside. Sauté the onion and garlic in the remaining oil in the pan over medium heat until softened, 3–4 minutes. Add the quince and simmer for 3 minutes.

Turn up the heat. Pour in the wine and let it evaporate. Stir in the orange juice, chicken stock, cinnamon stick, and honey. Simmer over low heat until the sauce has reduced a little, about 10 minutes. Return the pork to the pan and simmer until cooked through, about 10 minutes. Stir in the parsley. Season with salt and pepper. Serve hot.

SERVES 4 • PREPARATION 20 MIN. • COOKING 40 MIN. • LEVEL 2

17 pork chops
with gremolata

Pork Chops
- 16 cherry tomatoes, halved
- 4 tablespoons (60 ml) extra-virgin olive oil
- 1 small bunch chives, finely chopped
- 4 pork loin chops, bone-in
- Finely grated zest and freshly squeezed juice of 1 unwaxed lemon
- 1 tablespoon Dijon mustard
- 1 teaspoon honey
- Salt and freshly ground black pepper

Gremolata
- Finely grated zest of 2 unwaxed lemons
- 1/2 cup (25 g) finely chopped fresh parsley
- 2 cloves garlic, finely chopped

Pork Chops Preheat the oven to 400°F (200°C/gas 6). Put the tomatoes on a baking sheet and drizzle with 1 tablespoon of oil. Roast for 10 minutes. Sprinkle with the chives. Keep warm. Heat 1 tablespoon of oil in a large frying pan over high heat. Add the chops and sear for 1 minute on each side. Transfer to a baking dish. Mix the remaining 2 tablespoons of oil, lemon zest and juice, mustard, and honey in a small bowl. Drizzle over the chops and season with salt and pepper. Bake until cooked through, 10–15 minutes. Let rest for 5 minutes.

Gremolata Mix the lemon zest, parsley, and garlic in a small bowl. Sprinkle the gremolata over the chops. Serve hot with the roasted tomatoes on the side.

SERVES 4 • PREPARATION 20 MIN. • COOKING 20–25 MIN. • LEVEL 1

18 sicilian stuffed veal roll

- 4 ounces (120 g) ground (minced) lean beef or veal
- 8 ounces (250 g) highly flavored pork sausage meat
- 1 large egg, beaten
- 1/2 cup (60 g) freshly grated pecorino cheese
- 1 tablespoon finely chopped fresh parsley
- 1 small onion, finely chopped
- 2 cloves garlic, finely chopped
- Salt and freshly ground black pepper
- 1 1/2 pounds (750 g) lean beef from top round, rib, or chuck (topside, sirloin, or chuck), in a single layer
- 8 ounces (250 g) prosciutto (Parma) ham or ham, sliced
- 4 slices pancetta, chopped
- 3 hard-boiled eggs
- 4 ounces (120 g) provolone cheese, cut into thin strips
- 4 tablespoons (60 ml) extra-virgin olive oil
- 1/2 cup (120 ml) dry red wine
- 1 tablespoon tomato paste (concentrate), diluted in 1 cup (250 ml) hot water

Mix the ground beef and sausage meat in a large bowl. Add the beaten egg, pecorino, parsley, onion, garlic, salt, and pepper, and combine well. Place the slice of beef flat between 2 sheets of parchment paper and beat gently with a meat tenderizer until about 1/4 inch (5 mm) thick. Be careful not to tear it.

Lay the meat out flat and cover with the prosciutto and pancetta. Spread the ground meat mixture over the top, leaving a narrow border around the edge.

Slice the pointed ends off the eggs and place them "nose to tail" down the middle of the meat. Lay the provolone cheese on either side of the eggs. Carefully roll up, bringing one "long" side over the eggs. Tie with string at regular intervals.

Heat the oil in a large, flameproof casserole, and carefully brown the meat roll all over. Pour the wine over the top and cook, uncovered, until it has evaporated. Add the diluted tomato paste. Cover and simmer over very low heat for about 1 hour, turning several times.

Just before serving, remove the string and transfer to a heated serving platter. Carve at table into slices about 3/4 inch (2 cm) thick, spooning some of the cooking liquid over each serving.

SERVES 6 · PREPARATION 30 MIN. · COOKING 1 1/4 HR. · LEVEL 2

19 beef steaks
with sweet potatoes & mushrooms

- 1½ pounds (750 g) sweet potatoes, peeled and diced
- 2 tablespoons butter
- ¼ cup (60 ml) milk
- Salt
- 8 ounces (250 g) mushrooms, thinly sliced
- 4 scallions (spring onions), thinly sliced
- 2 cloves garlic, finely chopped
- 4 tablespoons (60 ml) extra-virgin olive oil
- 1 cup (250 ml) light (single) cream
- 3 tablespoons freshly squeezed lemon juice
- 1 tablespoon fresh thyme leaves
- 4 beef fillet steaks

Cook the sweet potatoes in a large pot of salted boiling water until tender, 10–15 minutes. Drain well and return to the pan. Mash with the butter and milk.

Sauté the mushrooms, scallions, and garlic in 2 tablespoons of oil in a large frying pan over medium heat until softened, 3–4 minutes. Stir in the cream, lemon juice, thyme, and salt. Bring to a boil. Simmer over low heat until thickened, about 1 minute.

Heat the remaining oil in a large frying pan over high heat. Cook the steaks for 5–10 minutes, until cooked to your liking. Serve hot with the vegetables.

SERVES 4 • PREPARATION 15 MIN. • COOKING 20–30 MIN. • LEVEL 1

20 rib of lamb
with garlic mash

Lamb
- 2 tablespoons extra-virgin olive oil
- 8 lamb rib chops
- Salt and freshly ground black pepper
- 2 tablespoons finely chopped thyme leaves
- 1¼ cups (300 ml) dry white wine
- 1¼ cups (300 ml) chicken stock
- Ripe tomatoes, to serve

Garlic Mash
- 1½ pounds (750 g) potatoes, peeled and diced
- ¼ cup (60 ml) milk
- 2 tablespoons extra-virgin olive oil
- 2 cloves garlic, finely chopped
- Salt and freshly ground black pepper

Lamb Preheat the oven to 350ºF (180ºC/gas 4). Heat the oil in a frying pan and brown the chops for 2 minutes on each side. Transfer to a baking dish. Season with salt, pepper, and thyme. Add half the wine and stock and bake for 20–30 minutes.

Garlic Mash Cook the potatoes until tender. Drain and mash with the milk, oil, garlic, salt, and pepper.

Remove the chops from the oven, cover, and let rest. Add the remaining wine and stock to the pan. Cook over medium heat until the liquid has reduced by one-third, 4–5 minutes. Serve hot with the mash, pan juices, and tomatoes.

SERVES 4 • PREPARATION 30 MIN. • COOKING 40 MIN. • LEVEL 2

index

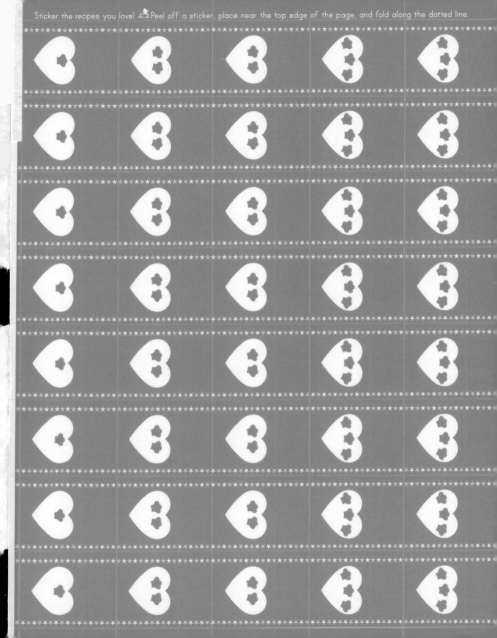